# Experience, Opportunity, and Developing Your Career

# HBR Work Smart Series

*Rise faster with quick reads,*
*real stories, and expert advice.*

It's not easy to navigate the world of work when you're exploring who you are and what you want in life. How do you translate your interests, skills, and education into building a career you love?

The **HBR Work Smart Series** features the topics that matter to you most in your early career, including being yourself at work, collaborating with (sometimes difficult) colleagues and bosses, managing your mental health, and weighing major job decisions. Each title includes chapter recaps and links to video, audio, and more. The HBR Work Smart books are your practical guides to stepping into your professional life and moving forward with confidence.

### Books in the series include:

*Authenticity, Identity, and Being Yourself at Work*

*Bosses, Coworkers, and Building Great Work Relationships*

*Boundaries, Priorities, and Finding Work-Life Balance*

*Experience, Opportunity, and Developing Your Career*

**WORK
SMART**

*Tips for Navigating
Your Career*

# Experience, Opportunity, and Developing Your Career

**HARVARD BUSINESS
REVIEW PRESS**
Boston, Massachusetts

Copyright 2024 Harvard Business School Publishing Corporation

All rights reserved

Printed in the United States of America

10 9 8 7 6 5 4 3 2 1

No part of this publication may be reproduced, stored in or introduced into a retrieval system, or transmitted, in any form, or by any means (electronic, mechanical, photocopying, recording, or otherwise), without the prior permission of the publisher. Requests for permission should be directed to permissions@harvardbusiness.org, or mailed to Permissions, Harvard Business School Publishing, 60 Harvard Way, Boston, Massachusetts 02163.

The web addresses referenced in this book were live and correct at the time of the book's publication but may be subject to change.

Library of Congress Cataloging-in-Publication Data

Names: Harvard Business Review Press, issuing body.
Title: Experience, opportunity, and developing your career / Harvard Business Review.
Description: Boston, Massachusetts : Harvard Business Review Press, [2024] | Series: HBR work smart series | Includes index.
Identifiers: LCCN 2023051856 (print) | LCCN 2023051857 (ebook) | ISBN 9781647827052 (paperback) | ISBN 9781647827069 (epub)
Subjects: LCSH: Career development. | Decision making.
Classification: LCC HF5381 .E857 2024 (print) | LCC HF5381 (ebook) | DDC 650.1—dc23/eng/20231204
LC record available at https://lccn.loc.gov/2023051856
LC ebook record available at https://lccn.loc.gov/2023051857

ISBN: 978-1-64782-705-2
eISBN: 978-1-64782-706-9

The paper used in this publication meets the requirements of the American National Standard for Permanence of Paper for Publications and Documents in Libraries and Archives Z39.48-1992.

# CONTENTS

SECTION 4

# How Do I Decide What's Next?

SECTION 5

# What If I Don't Want a Traditional
# Career Path?

# What Does It Mean to Have a Career?

by Mimi Aboubaker

Finding your footing in the early stages of your career can be daunting. You're no longer a student following a curriculum developed by someone else. Instead, you're an individual carving your own path in a world of infinite possibilities. You can choose to fear that freedom, or you can feel excited by it. The life and career you want is in your control.

I know it probably doesn't feel that way right now—I've been in your shoes. But writing this as a 28-year-old who has made a few career transitions herself, I can assure you that you have more power than you think. To harness it, I recommend thinking through three questions: What does it mean to have a career? Do you even want one? And why is it important to think about your options now?

Let's start with the first question: What does it even mean to have a career? To find your answer, you first need to understand the difference between a career and a job. Romantic relationships can be a good analogy here. Jobs are like dates. They serve a short-term objective or need—this can be getting your foot in the door, gaining stability, building credibility, and more. A career, on the other hand, is more like a relationship. In a career, various chapters of your life are bound by a commitment to something greater—a domain, an industry, or your expertise. Not every date will lead to a relationship, the same way not every job will lead to a career. A relationship will comprise many dates (aka jobs), activities, and challenging periods, just like a career. And while there's nothing wrong with making your way through life with a string of unconnected jobs, it's important to make that choice consciously.

That brings us to our second question: Do you even want a career? If you're reading this book, odds are you're at least a little interested in the concept of developing one. Are you excited to plan out a future based on your interests and goals? Do you have personal development aspirations and skills you're eager to learn? If so, working toward building a career is a good choice.

And finally, why is it important to think about your career at this point in your life? If you're just getting started in your career, you've got plenty of time to build it, right? While career development is a lifelong process, the groundwork you lay in the early days can actually have a huge impact on your future. I don't say this to scare you; I say it to encourage you.

In her TED Talk, Meg Jay, a clinical psychologist and the author of *The Defining Decade*, says, "Eighty percent of life's most defining moments take place by age 35. That means that eight out of 10 of the decisions and experiences and aha moments that make your life what it is will have happened by your mid-thirties."

It's also known that the first 10 years of your career predict your lifetime earnings.[1] But it's not just about building a sturdy foundation of good, high-paying jobs—your early career is also the time to create a strong internal foundation.

Your internal foundation is an amalgamation of who you really are as a person, the goals you have for yourself, and the habits and skills you choose to foster. Building one is all about self-discovery. What do you really want out of your career? What patterns in your behavior are holding you back? What are your nonnegotiables? The first chapter in this book, "Values, Passion, and Purpose," by Irina Cozma, can help you get started on answering these questions. This foundation is what will guide you on your path and help you make confident decisions throughout your career.

If all of this sounds a little overwhelming, that's OK. It was for me too when I was just starting out. My parents were refugees, and I walked into college without a roadmap. It wasn't until I landed my first internship that I really began developing my own internal foundation—refining my aspirations, working on my skills, and reflecting on my progress.

My first internship was at Prada's corporate office supporting logistics. I had always been interested in the business side of the fashion industry, so I was excited to get some actual experience with it. But in that internship, I quickly learned that the day-to-day work was not as dynamic as I'd wanted. Looking for more variety in my responsibilities, I landed a role at a consumer technology startup where I enjoyed the fast pace and diverse work. Still, something was missing—I wanted more stability.

These internships were my vehicle for building a personal foundation. Through these tangible experiences, I came to better understand my career-related values—I needed variety but also stability. I discovered my passion for the fashion industry, while also refining my abilities to adapt and deal with ambiguity. And I understood my goals—I was ready to move forward in my career and try something new.

When I began looking for my next opportunity, I used this foundation to help me decide between working at an emerging fashion brand or in finance. I had two amazing offers, one from Madewell and one from Morgan Stanley. So I asked myself: Which internship resonated most with my goals? What opportunity would I consider "the one that got away" if I didn't take it? Morgan Stanley came out on top. It turned out to be the right decision for me: I enjoyed finance and shifted to a different division for my next internship at Goldman Sachs. Investment banking offered the variety I'd been seeking since my first internship at Prada, as I was able to work on deals with multiple companies at the same time. And after all these internships, I eventually plunged into entrepreneurship—the ultimate application of my adaptability and flexibility.

None of these decisions was easy for me but getting to know myself through these experiences helped tremendously. As you begin to make thoughtful decisions about your career, I encourage you to continue building and leaning on your foundation, too. Check out chapter 11, "How to Make Better Decisions About Your Career," by Timothy Yen, for even more wisdom on this topic.

My story is just one of many you'll hear as you move through your career. You'll be exposed to a seemingly never-ending flow of career advice from your friends, family, colleagues, and of course, the internet—and everyone will seem to have it all figured out.

It's important to remember that not every piece of advice you hear about building you career will be helpful for you and your unique path (including some of my advice in this introduction). I hope as you read this book and navigate your professional life that you'll ask yourself the right questions and seek other feedback and opinions before making any moves. That's where having a network with diversity of perspectives and worldviews can be helpful—section 3 of this book is completely focused on how to build that network and mobilize them throughout your career journey.

Naturally, this means you will receive conflicting advice. For every person who made one choice, there's a person who made the opposite, and their perspectives will reflect these differences. That's why when I receive advice, I always ask myself: "What is this person's theory of success as a professional?" Most people have one whether they are aware of it or not. When providing feedback, it may come across like "Here's what worked for me" or "Here's what I did, and I regret it, so I'm advising something else." In chapter 15, "Four Pieces of Career Advice It's OK to Ignore," Tomas Chamorro-Premuzic also shares some guidance that can help you sort through the noise.

There are as many perspectives as there are experiences. In these pages you will find just a few. This book aims to be your guide as you navigate these early years and the growing pains of developing as a professional. It recognizes that the path to career success and fulfillment is not linear and that there is no definitive blueprint to follow. While there may be no single correct way to approach your career, you have the power to define your path based on your unique priorities, beliefs, and goals. In the chapters that follow, we will delve into the intricacies of career planning, job searching, networking, and the development of vital skills that will serve you well on your professional path.

So, let's begin this journey, armed with the understanding that your career is yours to define and yours to create. It's time to build your foundation.

# What Kind of Career Do I Want?

# 1

# Values, Passion, and Purpose

by Irina Cozma

When it comes to developing your career, you've heard the advice: Define your values, follow your passion, and find your purpose. But we all know following this advice isn't as easy as it sounds.

Identifying and understanding our values, passion, and purpose takes introspection and self-discovery. It requires us to examine our beliefs and motivations to gain clarity on what truly matters to us. And that's only the first step.

Once you understand what you actually want, it's another challenge to apply those aspirations to your career. Should you follow your passion or purpose? What if your values clash with your dream job? Is there a way to align your vision of a fulfilling career with the job market?

The only way to answer these questions is to truly understand the concepts of values, passion, and purpose, clarify your own perspective on each, and reflect on what they mean for you and your career.

# Values

Think of your values as the foundation for your passion and purpose—they define what is important to you and thereby can influence the passions you pursue and the purpose you seek to fulfill.

Your values are your answers to questions like "What is important for you in life?" or "What are your nonnegotiables?" Having an answer to these questions will bring clarity and direction when it comes to making decisions about your career and can help you balance when you feel frustrated or overwhelmed.

## Defining your values

To define your values, start by writing down the things in your life that matter to you most. Maybe it's friends, family, financial stability, creativity, sustainability—it's entirely up to you.

As you think of your list, it's important to be honest with yourself and focus on what is truly fundamental for you. Don't worry about what values will make you look good in the eyes of others—you never have to show anyone your list if you don't want to.

Once you have a list of words, it's important to also define what those words mean. You're not looking for the textbook definition; you're looking for an explanation of each value that is useful to you. For example, the way I define my value of happiness (the joy in the process of what I am doing) might be different from how you would define it.

Know that it might take time to find and stabilize your values. It took me a year of ongoing reflection before I felt firm on mine. You might start with a set of values and, months later, end up with a very different list. And it's likely that they will change as your grow in your life and career.

Even so, it's important that once you've defined your values you memorize them. Here is a test for yourself: If I woke you up in the middle of the night and asked you what your values are, would you be able to list them? If you can, you're more likely to use them in an effective manner.

## Using your values

Finding and defining your values requires hard work, but that is just the beginning. Values are not just abstract concepts; they should manifest in your actions, decisions, and behaviors. When your values are in alignment with your actions, you will experience greater satisfaction and authenticity. To reap the benefits of value identification, you also need to live by them day in and day out.

Let's consider the hypothetical example of Val, a recent graduate. One of Val's core values is freedom. For her, freedom is about having independence in her actions and decision-making. This is a nonnegotiable for her. She found that when she was micromanaged in her internships, she would leave feeling unhappy and underutilized. People told her that this is just what it's like when you're early in your career—you need to follow the rules if you want to advance. She understood that she might not have total freedom to pursue the exact career or roles she wanted, but she knew it'd be possible to find a job that would allow her the freedom to create initiatives or act on her ideas. When she began interviewing for jobs, she made it a point to ask her interviewers questions about how tasks are delegated, how new ideas are processed, and what room there would be for growth. Based on their answers, she was able to weed out organizations and managers that were likely to infringe on her value of freedom.

# Passion

Passion is what drives you to explore and engage in activities aligned with your values. Fundamental to passion is the strong and intense emotional drive that fuels its pursuit. It's the deep, fervent interest and enjoyment you derive from a particular activity, cause, or field.

And it's this emotion that often creates a high level of commitment to one's passion, even when times are hard. Take the many artists that continue to pursue their passion for art even if they never see the financial benefits during their lifetimes.

## Finding your passion

Passion often arises from within, driven by personal interests and desires. It's something you do because you genuinely love it, not necessarily because of external rewards or expectations. When you're passionate about something, you're naturally drawn to it, and the mere act of engaging in that activity or pursuing that interest becomes intrinsically rewarding.

What activities or pursuits in your life bring you a sense of joy and fulfillment just by engaging in them without any external rewards or pressures? Will you still do that thing even if nobody is watching or nobody will ever find out about it? If so, that is an indicator that you are truly passionate about it.

Keep in mind that you can have multiple passions in different areas of your life. For example, you may be passionate about painting, cooking, and environmental conservation. It can feel overwhelming to have multiple passions but know that you don't have to choose (unless you really want to). You can prioritize and re-prioritize them and make space for all of your passions in different proportions and at different times throughout your life. You may choose one to pursue in your career and focus on others outside of work. Or you may follow one passion at the beginning of your career and make a shift later in order to satisfy a different one.

## Using your passion

Knowing what you're passionate about can guide you in many different ways—from helping you find a career you'll love, to deciding on what moves to make on your path, to balancing your work and life.

Take the hypothetical example of Nisha. For as long as she could remember, Nisha's friends felt comfortable talking to her about their problems, and Nisha loved being that sounding board for them. She was deeply passionate about helping others and knew she wanted to pursue a career connected to people.

When the time came for her to choose a career path, she resisted her family's suggestion of going into finance and insisted on exploring a career where she could directly work to support others. She learned more about psychology and discovered that being a therapist closely aligned with her passion. This helped guide her as she made decisions about her college major, whether or not to attend graduate school, and what roles would be fulfilling.

# Purpose

Purpose is a broader and more profound concept that encapsulates how your values and passions come together.

It is your deeper reason for existence—it's a sense of meaning and direction in life that goes beyond personal enjoyment or fulfillment. Purpose often involves contributing to the greater good or serving a cause larger than yourself.

## Discovering your purpose

In order to find your purpose, ask yourself questions like "What do I believe is the ultimate reason for my existence?" or "What social or environmental issues do I feel strongly about and in what ways can my skills, passions, or resources contribute to addressing these issues?" These are big questions that might require time to process, so don't rush.

Your purpose will likely be more focused and singular compared to your passion. It represents a specific, overarching goal or mission—it's not a vague notion, but a clear and concrete objective that gives your life direction and meaning.

Think of your purpose as a mission statement for your life. For example, somebody's purpose might be to alleviate poverty in their community by providing financial resources to micro-entrepreneurs. In that case, they might target jobs in banking or other financial institutions so they can learn the system from the inside.

## Using your purpose

Like your values, your purpose can help guide your actions and serve as a constant reference point for decision-making in your career. It can be a guidepost for long-term planning, helping you understand your career in the context of what you ultimately want to achieve or the legacy you want to leave behind.

Take the hypothetical example of Paola, who identified her purpose as improving accessibility for people with disabilities. Paola was unhappy in her career, so when it came time to rethink her path, she considered her purpose. Her passion for nature also drew her focus to accessibility at national parks, so she began thinking through ways to pursue this opportunity. She could try to find a job directly in the National Park System. She could work for an advocacy group or the government to influence policies and funding. Or she could work for a company that designs infra-structure for people with disabilities. Given these options, she also considered her values—which path would allow her to also fulfill her values of financial stability and family?

Know that using your purpose for career decision-making may require you to prioritize your mission over short-term gains or comforts. Make sure you're clear on your nonnegotiables (your values) and the sacrifices you're willing to make to fulfill your purpose.

## Harmony and Tension Between Values, Passion, and Purpose

In summary, values are your nonnegotiable foundation, passion is about what excites and motivates you, and purpose is your deeper reason for existence. These concepts are deeply interconnected, and aligning them will give you the best chance at having a fulfilling life and career.

But having perfect alignment isn't always possible. It's likely that you'll encounter challenges in trying to live by your values, pursue your passion, and find your purpose. They may clash with each other—you may value financial security, but your passion is playing live music. They may clash with your current skills—your passion is video game development, but you didn't go to school for computer science. Or they may clash with the current job market—your purpose is to fight poverty and leave the world better than you found it, but finding a nonprofit job is harder than you expected.

Still, there are steps you can take to get closer to that alignment. If you are an accountant who enjoys playing music, you can get a job as an accountant in a music production company and play music on the weekends. If you're in sales but want to develop video games, you can get a sales job at a video game company while building your skills. And if you're looking to make a difference in the world while still making money, consider a job that can offer you financial stability and the ability to donate to nonprofits.

As you navigate advice around your career and applying these concepts, know that it's OK not to have all of them perfectly defined or aligned. You may need to prioritize them based on what's most useful to you in this current moment. There will be times when your values are driving you forward, and other times it will be your passion or purpose.

The truth is, *values*, *passion*, and *purpose* are just words—they will impact your life depending on the meaning you assign to them. It's up to you to discover what they mean for you and your career.

## QUICK RECAP

When it comes to developing your career, you've heard the advice: Define your values, follow your passion, and find your purpose. But what do these concepts actually mean?

- Values are the foundation for your passion and purpose— they define what is important to you, and they should manifest in your actions, decisions, and behaviors.

- Passion is what drives you to explore and engage in activities aligned with your values. Your passion can help you find a career you'll love and decide what career moves to make.

- Purpose encapsulates how your values and passions come together. It is your deeper reason for existence. It can be a helpful guidepost for long-term career planning.

---

Adapted from "Values, Passion, or Purpose—Which Should Guide Your Career?" on hbr.org, October 23, 2023.

Should you choose your passion over your paycheck?
Check out this article and video:

# How Do I Actually Build a Career?

# Create a Career Portfolio (Not a Career Path)

by April Rinne

Every four years or so, something inside me shifts. I get restless and want to learn something new or apply my skills in a new way. It's as though I shed a professional skin and start over, fresh.

In my twenties, I got all kinds of flak for this. When I decided to guide hiking trips rather than join a consulting firm, my peers said that my résumé made no sense. When I opted to defer graduate school to travel in India, my mentors questioned my seriousness and said my professional future could crash.

I felt like something was wrong with me because I was interested in so many things while my friends were laser-focused on climbing the corporate ladder. It's not that I wasn't disciplined or willing to work hard. There was just too much worth learning and doing. To settle on one pursuit seemed like a mistake.

Today, the world has changed in some amazing and profound ways. Broadening your career focus and professional identity is no longer seen as a negative. It's celebrated. The macro forces driving the future of work demand independent and adaptable thinkers. As you start to think about your career, or continue to develop it, try stepping away from the idea of it needing to be a path, and start thinking of it as a portfolio instead.

## What Is a Career Portfolio?

A career portfolio is a different way to think about, talk about, and—most important—craft your professional future in order to navigate our ever-changing world of work with purpose, clarity, and flexibility.

Whereas a career path tends to be a singular pursuit (climb the ladder in one direction and focus on what is straight ahead), a career portfolio represents your vast and diverse professional journey (including the various twists and turns made by choice or by circumstance).

My portfolio, as an example, includes author, speaker, futurist, adviser, lawyer, hiking guide, global development executive, investor, and yoga practitioner. Each of these identities took time to develop. Some of them included traditional jobs, while others meant self-employment, pro bono work, and sweat equity investments. Many are roles I've been in simultaneously and longer than my usual four-year stint, though my periodic urge to add another to the list continues unabated.

As you begin to build your own portfolio, you don't have to have everything figured out. In fact, it's probably better if you don't. That's the beauty of a portfolio. Because it's not focused on a singular end, it gives you more space—and frankly, more wisdom—to test out different things and find your way.

# How Do I Build a Career Portfolio?

The first thing to remember is: You already have a career portfolio—even if you don't realize it, and even if you've never had a paid job. Start by identifying what's in it.

While your portfolio can include traditional paid jobs, don't limit yourself. Think bigger. Your portfolio is created by you, rather than determined for you by someone else (like a bunch of hiring managers). It reflects your professional identity and potential. It includes your unique combination of skills, experiences, and talents that can be mixed, matched, and blended in different ways.

If you've helped care for your siblings, led a team of online gamers, or done community outreach, include these activities in your portfolio. In fact, include any role or activity in which you've created value and served others: freelance roles, volunteering, community service, side hustles, passion projects, hobbies, exchanges, parenting, supporting your family and friends, and so on.

Your portfolio should also include experiences and capabilities that are customarily left off your résumé, yet fundamental to who you are. For example, my status as an orphan, globetrotter, insatiable handstander, and mental-health advocate are all essential components of my portfolio. These identities help power the work that I do.

How you keep track of your portfolio is a matter of personal preference. I suggest creating a simple list to start. But because the real value of your portfolio is in its diversity, you'll want to make connections between the things that are in it.

Personally, I draw my portfolio: It looks like a network with many different nodes. As I add new skills, roles, or experiences, I add those elements to my drawing.

## What Are the Benefits of a Career Portfolio?

Practically speaking, a career portfolio typically leads to greater ownership of your career, because unlike a job that someone else gives you (and determines the scope of, and whether you will advance), a portfolio can't simply be taken away. It is yours forever.

Similarly, a career portfolio gives you a unique professional identity that evolves alongside you (and isn't roiled to the core if you lose a job, shift gears, or even start over from time to time). It's naturally aligned with lifelong learning and meant to help you expand your professional community and access to leadership opportunities. Consider your portfolio part of your strategy to be "un-automatable," too.

Over time, the value of your portfolio will increase by your ability to cross-pollinate: to combine and weave together skills from your different experiences in order to gain new insights, tackle new problems, diversify income sources, and serve in new ways.

In a world of uncertainty, people who can expand their thinking beyond boxes, silos, or sectors will be in demand. Those who make an effort to build a career portfolio now will be more prepared to pitch themselves for (and even create) new opportunities, as they will be well-practiced at making creative connections between their various skills and the skills required of the jobs they most wish to pursue.

## How Do I Use My Portfolio to Land the Roles I Want?

It's key to be clear about how your portfolio enables you to be proactive, to learn, and to contribute in ways that a traditional career path would not. I call this your *portfolio narrative.*

Employers are hungry to hire talent with nontraditional backgrounds, but they often need help. Your portfolio narrative is the link—it is the story you tell to make connections between the skills people are hiring for and the skills you have developed through the breadth of your experience.

For example, when I was a hiking and biking guide, some people said my career looked frivolous (or even like "too much fun"). What they didn't see was that as a guide, not only was I usually working 18-hour days—first up and last to bed—but I was also learning how to project manage, accommodate differences, balance budgets, build teams, ensure safety, forge lifetime friendships, and spark joy. I didn't have a fancy title or earn very much, but I got a practical mini-MBA on the trail and perspective that would shape the rest of my life.

Often, I've had to fill in these gaps for others. Being able to explain why my experience was valuable in this way didn't just shape my portfolio—it helped me stand out from other candidates when I applied for jobs.

Telling a good portfolio narrative requires understanding how the different things in your portfolio enhance one another. How does your combination of skills give you an edge? I like to think of this as "$1+1=11$": Your combination of skills is far more valuable than any of them on their own. When answering interview questions, for instance, share a story about how you applied skills you learned in two very different settings to solve one specific problem.

. . .

The future of work is full of uncertainty. It's hard to know what to do or to trust that things will work out. But taking ownership of your portfolio is something that you can control, and you can start today. Your future will thank you.

## QUICK RECAP

As you think about your career, try stepping away from the idea that it needs to be a path, and start thinking of it as a portfolio instead.

- Whereas a career path tends to be a singular pursuit (climbing the ladder), a career portfolio represents your diverse professional journey.

- While your portfolio can highlight traditional paid jobs, it should also encompass your professional identity, skills, experiences, and talents.

- Make connections between the experiences and skills in your portfolio. This will help you create a narrative around your experience and give you an advantage when pitching yourself to potential employers.

---

Adapted from "Why You Should Build a 'Career Portfolio' (Not a 'Career Path')" on hbr.org, October 13, 2021.

Looking for another way to think about your career path?
Watch this video:

## 3

# How to Build a Career You Won't Hate

by Michelle Gibbings

Whether you're just getting started in your career, or are ready to take the next step, you need to approach your career goals strategically. You need intention, but also flexibility, to move forward—you need a career guide.

A career guide is a well-thought-out plan highlighting what it will take to progress your career in ways that you find truly meaningful. This approach has served me (and my clients) well throughout my time in the corporate world and now as an executive coach helping others make the leaps that will advance their careers.

## Create Your Own Career Guide

Your guide will include four parts. Each is meant to challenge you to think critically about what you want and where you should focus your energy. The ultimate goal is to identify and take steps that will help you align your career with your deeper purpose and skills.

## Part 1: Write down your current career traps

Have you ever had a job, internship, or class that you felt trapped in? Maybe you knew something was off or wasn't working, but you struggled to pinpoint why. This feeling is often caused by what I call career traps—patterns of thinking or behaviors that we practice because they're familiar to us, even though they can negatively impact us. It can take a crisis—a pandemic, getting fired, painful boredom, burnout, loss, or a significant illness–for us to stop, reflect, and recognize the career traps that might be getting in our way.

Don't wait for that to happen. Based on my experience, there are five common traps people fall into. Be proactive by challenging yourself to consider if you've struggled with any of these traps, and which ones may impede your progress.

- *Ambition trap:* You're a high performer who is used to success. You worry that if you slow down you'll stop achieving. Not knowing how to dial it back, your solution is to work harder when the pressure at work rises.

- *Expectation trap:* You continually strive to meet other people's expectations. Consequently, admitting that you're struggling and overworked is ego shattering. You worry that people will think less of you if you acknowledge you are burned out or unable to cope.

- *Busyness trap:* You enjoy being busy and consider it a part of your identity. For you, work always comes first. As a result, you struggle to say no, slow down, or switch off. You likely regularly sacrifice time with loved ones and your health for your job.

- *Translation trap:* You've worked hard to get to where you are, yet the happiness you thought you'd find eludes you. You have all the hallmarks of success, but you feel like you have lost your way because your role doesn't fulfill or inspire you. Nor does it align with your purpose. At the same time, you worry about changing directions because you believe that your current job is all you know.

- *Adrenaline trap:* You run your life on adrenaline, not taking enough time to care for your mind, body, and spirit. You are run down and overworked. You say to yourself, "I'll take a break tomorrow," but tomorrow ends up being just as busy. You have forgotten that putting your self-care needs first is a critical act of leadership and crucial for a sustainable career.

Avoiding these traps in your career (and getting out of them) involves making deliberate trade-offs, and deciding on those trade-offs will become easier when you are clear on what matters to you.

## Part 2: Define your purpose

Your purpose is your why—the reason you do what you do. For some of us, it may be to lead a happy and healthy life. For others, it may be to create a life filled with learning and passing on those lessons. Purpose can center around study, experimentation, and trying new things. It can involve serving our communities, taking risks, or venturing into the unknown. Whatever your purpose is, research shows that we can find meaning in our work by putting our why at the center of our decision-making.

So, what's *your* purpose? Answering this question isn't easy, and there's no magic formula. It's an iterative process that involves some soul searching. To start, pay attention to what matters to you and motivates you.

Ask yourself:

- What matters to me?

- What and who inspires me?

- When have I been the most motivated?

- What difference do I want to make through my work?

- When have I been most proud of who I am as a person?

When you answer these questions, consider both your personal and professional life. This holistic approach is essential because you can't divorce your work from the rest of your existence. A decision you make personally will affect you professionally (and vice versa).

Write down your responses and look for themes or common threads. If you are more of a visual thinker, you might even try creating Pinterest boards for each question. The objective is to capture your thoughts, feelings, moods, and impressions. Your ideas don't need to be perfectly formed, so long as they have meaning. Over time, ideas will percolate, bubble up, and the obvious answers will spill over. When that happens, you will know you have hit on something. It will feel right.

Once you know your purpose (which, by the way, can shift and change over time), you can be more intentional about dropping the habits that don't serve you (your career traps) and doing things that bring you closer to it. When picking a job or career path or saying yes to a new project, for example, you can ask yourself, "Does this align with what really matters to me? Does it get me one step closer to living a life aligned with my purpose?"

If the answer to those questions is yes, you know you're ready to move forward.

## Part 3: Document your unique skills and create your selling statement

Say you want to get a job that will stretch you, and you've found one that aligns with your purpose of always learning. To get that job, you'll need to demonstrate what makes you a good candidate, and more so, better than others who may be vying for that same job.

Take some time to identify your unique selling point (USP)— the skills and experiences that, combined, make you better than your competition.

To find your USP, try this exercise:

- Divide a sheet of paper into two columns (or use Google Sheets or a Word file).

- List the skills and competencies you know you have in one column. Include role-specific technical and functional skills (things like programming, design, or accounting), as well as non-role-specific competencies (such as problem-solving, relationship building, or creativity).

- For each item on your list, ask, "What value or benefit does this offer an employer?" and add your responses in the next column. For example, your digital skills may help an organization elevate its digital presence, or your strong relationship-building techniques may support a business looking to improve its customer engagement.

- Look at your experience and expertise and highlight your greatest strengths—the specific skills that make you an especially valuable candidate.

Once you've gathered all your data, use your analysis to start drafting your selling statement, a short explanation of who you are, what you stand for, and the value you can bring to any team, culture, or organization. Play with the words and sentences until you find a combination that accurately captures your essence.

Here are some short examples:

*Example 1:* I am an energetic sales professional committed to building strong and successful customer relationships. With a demonstrated record of identifying and nurturing potential leads and converting those into successful customer relationships, I create sustainable, high-quality revenue streams.

*Example 2:* I'm committed to making a difference by helping people learn and grow in their roles through my work. I'm skilled at creating a shared sense of purpose among my team members so we can deliver outcomes in a rapidly changing and complex operating environment. I do this by bringing the talents of each individual person to the forefront.

Your selling statement has multiple uses—you can use it as an elevator pitch for prospective employers and add it to your résumé or LinkedIn profile. Remember, though, crafting your statement isn't a one-and-done exercise. As you grow your skill sets and experience, you can and should revisit and rewrite it. Plus, what's valued by employers will change with time, so you want to ensure your USP is current, meaningful, and targeted.

## Part 4: Seize opportunities to expand yourself

It's important to always be on the lookout for opportunities that align with your purpose and skills. Write down a list of internal projects or teams you'd like to work on, organizations you'd be interested in applying to at some point, or volunteer opportunities you'd like to pursue. That way, when an opportunity arises that aligns with your purpose, goals, current skills, and the skills you need to build to move forward, you'll be ready. The key here is to be strategic about the process—you don't need to say yes to every opportunity.

And remember: Successful careers don't happen by accident or without help from others. You need great people around you to inspire, challenge, and support you along the way. It can also be helpful to write down a list of specific individuals or people with roles you'd like to learn more about that you're eager to get in touch with. This will help you further build your network and find opportunities that will move you forward. Having a broad and deep network can help you expand your mindset about what's possible, more readily learn about how your industry and profession are changing and identify where new opportunities are arising.

. . .

Now's the time to do the work. With your career guide drafted, your purpose at hand, and your attention focused, you're ready to move forward.

## QUICK RECAP

If you want to move forward in your career with intention, consider creating a career guide. Follow these steps:

- Identify your career traps, or the patterns of thinking that you practice because they're familiar, even though they negatively impact you.

- Define your purpose by asking yourself what matters to you and why you do what you do.

- Identify your unique selling point (USP)—the skills and experiences that make you better than your competition when applying for jobs.

- Write down a list of internal projects or teams you'd like to work on, organizations you'd be interested in applying to, or volunteer opportunities you'd like to pursue.

---

Adapted from content posted on hbr.org,
February 8, 2022.

# Five Ways to Figure Out If a Job Is Right for You

by Roxanne Calder

Have you ever landed a job or internship that you were so excited for, only to feel like accepting the offer was a mistake? You're not alone.

In a recent survey of 2,500 millennial and Gen Z applicants, 72% of respondents were surprised or regretted accepting a role because the position or company was very different from what they were led to believe it would be, and 41% said they would give the job just two to six months before leaving.[1]

Here's the thing: Just because a role seems like it will be the perfect fit doesn't mean it will be. And just because a job seems like it might help you advance in your career doesn't mean you should always take it.

Just as employers evaluate you, you should also be evaluating your potential employers. It's all about taking the time to know what the role will entail and how the organization will (or won't) align with your values, potential, and career goals.

# Apply to a Job, Even If You Don't Meet All Criteria

**by Janet T. Phan**

Imagine this: You log on to your favorite job posting website to look for a new role. As you scroll, you stumble upon a job that looks perfect! You're excited to apply based on the description, but then, your hopes and dreams are squashed by the "required skills" or "years of experience" section.

All too often, people don't apply for a new position simply because they don't hit every single one of the criteria included in the job description. Research shows that while men and women share similarities in how they browse and look for jobs, women are 16% less likely to apply to a job after viewing it, and also apply to 20% fewer jobs than men.[a] The reason? A report showed that women hold back if they don't meet 100% of the criteria, while men usually apply after meeting about 60%.[b] In both cases, those who don't apply usually hold back because they feel they won't be hired without checking off all the boxes, so why waste their time and energy?

This presents a big challenge, especially when most entry-level jobs still "require" a year or two of previous work experience. If you're just out of school or still new to the workforce, don't let this or other so-called requirements limit you. Instead, follow these tips:

- If you're a college graduate, count internships relevant to the role in your years of experience.

- If you're five years into your career, and the criteria asks for eight years, apply. This goes for all roles—there's typically two to three years of wiggle room when it comes to work experience.

- If you meet about 60% of the criteria, apply.

No matter the end result, remember: You'll never be considered if you don't apply. The key is getting that first interview. After that, it's up to you to craft your work history and experience into a story that convinces the hiring manager you're right for the role. Commit to showing up for yourself in this way. The reality is you won't land all the roles, but you might land one. And you'll never know if you don't try.

a. Deanne Tockey and Maria Ignatova, *Gender Insights Report: How Women Find Jobs Differently*, LinkedIn, n.d., https://business.linkedin.com/content/dam/me/business/en-us/talent-solutions-lodestone/body/pdf/Gender-Insights-Report.pdf.

b. Tara Sophia Mohr, "Why Women Don't Apply for Jobs Unless They're 100% Qualified, hbr.org, August 25, 2014, https://hbr.org/2014/08/why-women-dont-apply-for-jobs-unless-theyre-100-qualified.

---

Adapted from content posted on hbr.org, July 20, 2022.

So when you find a role you think will help you step up in your career, take these steps before accepting an offer to make sure it's the right move for you.

# 1. Validate the Job Description

Job descriptions, when used correctly, can provide you with great insights about a company or a role. They can clue you in on the responsibilities you would hold, reveal how your performance will be measured, and even help you evaluate your current skill sets.

Use platforms like LinkedIn or the company's website to start your research. On LinkedIn, view the profiles of people who might be working in similar roles at the organization. Their work history, background, and qualifications (skills and expertise) can help you get a realistic sense of the role and evaluate your own skill level. For instance, if you feel the employees you find are far less experienced than you, it might mean the role is too junior for you—despite the title. Or you may notice that you need to upskill to strengthen your application.

On occasion, a job description might use words or phrases that sound confusing or vague. For example, the phrase "conflict management" could mean anything from "communicating clearly with customers" to "leading complex projects" to "recovering from mistakes quickly." Similarly, a "senior" job title may not always equate to a managerial or high-level role depending on the size and structure of the company.

Keep in mind that—unfortunately—not all job descriptions provide an accurate representation of a role. Some may be outdated or pulled together perfunctorily. So, approach them with a critical mindset and don't be afraid to ask questions about the description during your interviews.

## 2. Pay Attention to the Company Culture

Every business has a culture: the values, habits, and behaviors that define their day-to-day work environment. If the culture is a good fit, you'll likely feel comfortable and confident bringing your whole self to work. If it's not a good fit, it may be more difficult for you to grow and learn in the role.

To understand a company's culture, pay attention to how they communicate with you from day one—the first email they send, the first phone call you have with their recruiters, your job interviews, and even follow-up emails. After each exchange, stop and consider how you feel. Are they transparent, genuine, and empathetic? What is the tone and demeanor of the people facilitating the process? Are they interested and eager to learn more about you? Nerves aside, is it easy to be yourself and ask questions?

If you're attending an in-person interview, observe your surroundings. Even when waiting in reception, strike up a conversation with employees who may be passing by. A lot can be uncovered through a three-minute chat.

During the interview itself, ask the hiring manager detailed questions about the environment, culture, and communication practices the team prefers. For example, if you're an introvert, you may want to understand how your potential boss collaborates with different personalities. You can ask:

- How are mistakes handled?

- How is success measured?

- How has the team resolved a conflict or a difficult situation in the past?

- How do managers communicate with and lead people from different backgrounds?

- How will I be supported if my boss works in a different time zone?

- What are the avenues for growth in this role?

- Will I be supported if I want to upskill?

Ask about employee turnover, internal promotions, and lateral moves—and with each question, probe the hiring manager for specific examples. (If their answers are vague, that may be a negative sign.) Pay attention to their language and tone. Do you mesh well? Would you feel comfortable with this person setting goals for you and giving you feedback? This goes for potential team members as well. Should you get the opportunity to meet them, ask yourself: Can I see myself working with and depending on these people?

## 3. Discuss Salary and Benefits

As soon as you can, determine if the salary of the role matches its market value. Websites like Glassdoor and Payscale usually have information about the market value of specific roles in different locations. You can also talk with friends and peers who work in similar fields or positions.

If the salary isn't disclosed in the job description, ask the Human Resources person facilitating the process about how compensation is determined. If you're directly in touch with the hiring manager, bring it up during the first interview. You'll need to walk a careful line—avoid coming off as money-hungry, but also show that you take compensation seriously and consider it an important aspect to consider.

Questions you can ask include:

- Will compensation be structured according to my previous income and experience?

- Does the company have internal salary bands or any external management consulting firm conducting research to determine fair pay?

- How are bonuses and benefits rolled out?

Don't forget about health insurance, childcare, pension contributions, parking, travel allowance, vacation, bonuses, parental leave, well-being and work-from-home policies, flexible schedules, and other benefits—these are just as important to consider as salary. Even if the pay is not competitive, robust and inclusive benefits can add to the overall compensation and, importantly, signal how the company values and takes care of its employees.

## 4. Conduct Your Own Background Checks on the Organization (and the Manager)

Most companies are going to check your references—and you should do the same for them. If joining a large organization or well-known brand, this information may be easier to gather.

Websites, articles, press releases, and annual reports will uncover a lot. You can also dig a little deeper to learn about their reputation and integrity by messaging former employees on LinkedIn. If the business is a startup or new venture, research the funding and investment to understand if the company is financially viable and has the potential to grow. When it comes to your potential boss, check out their LinkedIn profile, website, or other social media platforms. This will give you a look into their educational background and skills, as well as their views and values. Getting to know your potential coworkers better before actually starting a role may help you better understand the environment you could be working in.

## 5. Refocus on Your Career Goals

Your decision around whether to accept or decline an offer should at the end of the day be driven by your interests, values, and future goals. Envision where you see yourself at least two years from now. Do you want to work for a legacy brand? Do you want access to training and development? Do you want to progress quickly? More money? More free time? More purpose? There are no right or wrong answers.

During the interview process, share your goals with the hiring manager. This is a good way to determine if the organization can deliver on your expectations. For instance, if you want to pursue higher education in the future, ask if there is a work-study policy. If promotions are your motivator, ask how people on the team have grown and progressed. If you're looking to hone your technical skills and work with the best people in the business, ask about mentoring opportunities or development programs. You can even ask the manager what they expect of the role two years from now. How do these expectations align (or not align) with your goals? Being clear and transparent about your priorities during the interview process will help you make the best decision and avoid career roadblocks when starting a new job.

. . .

At first glance, this may seem like a lot of work. But the more you engage in the process, the more confident you will be in your career decisions. The workplace is now transforming into a place where we bring our whole selves, not just our skills and expertise—and both employees and employers are driving that change. You deserve to find a role and a company that works for you and your career goals just as much as you work for them.

## QUICK RECAP

Just as employers evaluate you, you should be evaluating your potential employers to ensure that a role will align with your goals. Here are five things you can do:

- Use platforms like LinkedIn to ensure the job description is accurate for the advertised role.

- To get a feel for company culture, ask questions during the interview process about how they typically handle mistakes, measure success, and support growth.

- Ask about compensation and benefits—fair pay and inclusive benefits can signal that the company values its employees.

- Check the company's references by reaching out to former employees on LinkedIn.

- Envision where you see yourself in two years. Share your goals with the hiring manager to make sure the organization can deliver on your expectations.

---

Adapted from content posted on hbr.org,
September 23, 2022.

Is it possible to turn any job into a job you'll love?
Listen to this podcast:

# 5

# Why You Should Take on More Stretch Assignments

by Jahna Berry

When you think about what success will look like for you in your career, what do you imagine? Maybe it's landing a role at the company of your dreams. Or maybe it's finally getting a job that will help you transition into a new industry.

Whatever comes to mind when you think about potential career wins, there's a good chance "taking on a stretch assignment" wasn't on your list. It's time to change that.

A stretch assignment is a project you take on in your role that requires skills or knowledge beyond your current level of development. The reason such projects can be so positive for your career growth is that they offer a great opportunity for you to learn new things, meet new people, and shine in a new arena.

This is also the exact reason why they can feel so scary. It can be terrifying to take on a project you're not totally equipped for or unsure if you can execute perfectly. But if you're willing to take the risk, and you do it well, taking on a stretch assignment can be the very thing that helps you move forward in your career.

Of course, the stakes are higher if you, like me, are queer, Black, a woman, or have other overlapping identities and work in an industry where you are a first or one of the few. Botching an unfamiliar task is one of the most common fears I've heard during my decade as a mentor and coach to rising leaders of color and queer managers. Considerable research shows that women, people of color, and members of the queer community are punished more heavily when they make mistakes.[1] This is true at every level of experience, from CEOs to students.[2] Those of us who share these identities know that a job setback or loss may be harder to recover from. It's no wonder we feel pressure to perform perfectly.

While systemic biases are real—and it's ultimately on leaders, lawmakers, voters, and industry watchdogs to tackle them—we are not powerless. Based on my own career and experience mentoring others, I can tell you that, despite the initial fear, taking on a stretch assignment is usually worth it. Many of the promotions I've had can be traced back to saying yes to these opportunities. Handling unfamiliar work is a skill that you can learn and refine.

Here's how to tackle your next stretch assignment and use the opportunity to reach your career goals.

## Recognize and Shift Your Negative Self-Talk

When you're starting a stretch project, it might be hard to not focus on everything that could go wrong. You may fear people will find out you don't know what you're doing. This is especially true for those of us who have overlapping identities or work in environments rife with microaggressions.

If you already feel pressure to perform perfectly, in a dark moment you may experience thoughts like "I don't belong here," "I can't do this," or "I'll mess this up." A key part of your success will depend on your ability to turn down the volume of the imposter in your head.

Earlier in my career, I had the opportunity to lead the daily morning news meeting at a media outlet where I worked. My job was to steer news coverage, making sure everyone's voice was heard, asking smart questions, and keeping the dozen or so attendees engaged and productive. Until that point in my career, I had most often seen men or white women play this high-profile role. It was rarely, if ever, owned by a woman of color. The first few weeks I led the meeting, my stomach was in knots every morning.

Today, I recognize that my initial unease was a natural feeling. I was the only Black editor in the newsroom. This was often a theme in my career: I've been the only Black intern, Black editor, Black manager, and so on.

A good way to shift your mindset is journaling. This strategy has worked for many of the leaders I coach. When you're feeling overwhelmed by self-doubt, pause and take some time to reflect. Write down all of the times that you tried something new and figured it out. It could be a skill you acquired at work that makes you proud, like public speaking, copywriting, or data analysis. It could also be something you learned outside of work, like a new language or how to make friends and build community in a new city.

Don't just jot down what you learned. Describe in detail any setbacks you faced, any fears you felt along the way, and how you overcame them. Reminding yourself of these wins will help you build confidence and give your mind the evidence it needs to prove that you're capable of taking on challenges.

Even now, as a chief operating officer, I sometimes use this practice in the face of new or challenging tasks that shake my confidence. Looking back at my journal entries helps me remember I can trust myself to eventually figure things out.

## Get Clarity

When taking on a stretch project, odds are you won't be given all of the information you need up front to be successful. That's the nature of stepping onto a new team or raising your hand for an assignment that's never been done. This lack of clarity can be especially difficult for those with overlapping identities.

Emerging BIPOC, female, and/or queer leaders working in predominantly white, male, heteronormative spaces are operating in environments that were not created with them in mind. This means you often have less access to stakeholders at the highest level of your organization than your white counterparts. You might also be less likely to have senior colleagues guiding and supporting you.

If this is your situation, you may sometimes find yourself late to pick up on nonverbal cues or jargon that your peers know well—simply because you have not been in the room. For instance, you may not initially know that a C-level executive always twirls her pen when she wants you to wrap up a presentation. Or you may not know that people are sharing key information in Slack channels you haven't been invited to. This guarding of knowledge can sometimes extend to the projects you take on, including stretch projects, which are more challenging by nature.

At the start of your stretch project, seek to gain clarity around your manager's expectations, important deadlines, specific goals you need to hit within those time frames, and any important stakeholders you need to keep in the loop along the way. Schedule some one-on-one time with your manager to thoroughly discuss these points. During your meeting, ask how you should communicate your progress, who needs updates by when, and what medium you should use to deliver information (in-person meetings, emails, quick Slack updates, and so forth). What decision points does your supervisor want to participate in? What team members, departments, or senior colleagues will the project impact? Most important, what does success look like?

For example, there may be a senior executive in another department who has unspoken or explicit authority over a part of your project. Once you know this, you can start to think strategically about their goals and anticipate the questions they may ask you as the project progresses. You can even plan to meet with them to learn more about their expectations.

With every milestone you hit, check in with your manager or stakeholders about the assignment's original goals, as many projects tend to evolve over time.

## Do a Listening Tour

You may initially feel hesitant or nervous to meet one-on-one with senior colleagues or executives. A listening tour is a good way to overcome that fear, build bridges with the different teams, and fast-track the knowledge you need to execute your stretch project.

At the start of the project, tell stakeholders and your manager that you plan to do a series of one-on-one meetings so you can get up to speed on the initiative. When you reach out, explain the project you're leading and what information you want to learn from them. Keep it short. You can say something like "I'm reaching out because I'm spearheading X initiative. I'm talking to all of the key stakeholders to learn as much as I can. You and your team are experts on X, and I'd love to touch base so I can learn more about how X works, how your team works, and how we can best collaborate."

Use your meeting to do three things: Communicate transparently that you are not an expert in the area yet; show a sincere interest in learning more; and give the people who are experts a chance to showcase what they know. Your goal isn't to immediately become an expert; it's to ask informed questions that will help you perform your role better. Try to ask similar questions in each meeting so that you can see patterns or other important information in your notes.

Here are a few questions that I like to ask during listening tours:

- How did you end up working here/on this project?

- What is your role and your team's role on this project?

- What should we stop doing? What should we keep doing?

- What is harder than it needs to be?

- How did we end up doing XYZ process this way?

- What are some things you're afraid I might get wrong?

- If you could wave a magic wand, what would you do?

- Who else should I talk to?

If the stakeholder shares their opinion but doesn't elaborate, follow up with something like, "Wow, that's an interesting observation. Why did you say that?" If they share a complex process that you find difficult to understand, explain that you're having a hard to time digesting their point, and ask them to re-explain it as if they are talking to a relative who doesn't work in the industry. This will help them communicate more clearly.

While asking follow-up questions may feel embarrassing—especially if you are an emerging leader and don't want people to doubt your abilities—the most important thing is that you understand how the pieces of your project fit together. Think of these conversations as an exciting opportunity to learn something new and to excel at your assignment.

When the conversation is over, thank the other person, and ask, "If I come across something I don't understand, may I reach out to you again?" People will appreciate your effort to educate yourself. No matter how senior they are, if this project and its success is important to them, they will want to support you and see you succeed.

## Trust Your Gut

As you work your way through this exciting assignment, remember to cut yourself some slack along the way. Research shows that expertise is probably not what your new team or collaborators value the most. In Google's internal research on managing, subject matter expertise ranked last on the list of top eight qualities that make a good manager.[3] What mattered more? Excelling at the core task the manager was entrusted with—managing the team.

So, if you've been asked to project manage a big initiative, focus most of your energy on stewarding that project with excellence. (There's probably a good chance you were chosen to steer a project on an unfamiliar topic *because* you are a strong project manager.)

A major component of leading with confidence is trusting your ability to figure things out. That might be hard at first, especially if you're an emerging BIPOC, female, and/or queer leader—your personal sense of safety at work may come from avoiding criticism or constantly code switching. But remember, this project is an opportunity to hone new skills. Focus on learning how to sift through information, discern the most important details, and leverage *your own expertise* to make decisions.

And remember: Don't let fear drive your decisions. Follow your intuition.

How do you distinguish the two? I tell my mentees to use an exercise called "I knew better," adapted from the work of life coach Shirin Eskandani.[4] Write down all of the times you had a hunch to do something, but against your better judgment you didn't do it. In the end, if you found yourself saying "I knew better," that initial hunch was your intuition.

When thinking back to that initial instinct, what did that inner knowing feel like in your body? Remember this, and the next time you have the intuition to do something, write it down. Note when you follow through and don't follow through. The goal of this exercise is to use these moments as data points so you can learn what your gut instinct feels like when you're stuck at a pivot point during your new project.

. . .

Taking on a project outside your area of expertise is a terrific way to grow as a leader. Like any opportunity, it will put you in a situation where you need to navigate discomfort. Take the risk and raise your hand for stretch assignments that catch your eye. It might take your career in a positive, unexpected direction.

## QUICK RECAP

Taking on a stretch assignment—a project that requires skills beyond your current level—can help you learn and grow in your career. Keep these tips in mind when taking one on:

- When you're feeling overwhelmed by self-doubt, write down all of the times that you tried something new and figured it out.

- At the very start of your project, seek to gain clarity from stakeholders about their expectations, important deadlines, and specific goals you need to hit.

- Don't let your fear of failing overcome your intuition. Think about all of the times you had a hunch but didn't follow it. Remember this feeling and trust it the next time it comes around.

Adapted from content posted on hbr.org, April 7, 2023.

What should you do when you're pushed outside of your
comfort zone at work? Listen to this podcast:

# Who Can Help?

# 6

# Want to Advance in Your Career? Build Your Own Board of Directors

by Susan Stelter

If you're reading this, chances are that you have a lot of questions about building a career. What path will fulfill your personal and professional needs? Should you be focused on making an impact or learning new skills? Is it better to find work-life balance or put in more hours to prove yourself?

When you're new to the workforce, these questions are hard to answer on your own—especially when things feel so uncertain. You may lack the information necessary to make a confident decision. You may be unsure of what the next steps should look like. You may even require more time to figure out your core values. Knowing what you want and how to go about getting it takes trial and error, and you'll likely need some help to figure things out.

You need a career board of directors.

The concept, originally proposed by Jan Torrisi-Mokwa in her book, *Building Career Equity*, is not the same as having multiple mentors. Traditionally, a mentor is a senior colleague or professional whose work you deeply admire. You may want to emulate their leadership style, learn from their experience, or follow in their footsteps. Mentorships are often formal, one-on-one relationships that can require a significant time commitment.

A career board of directors, on the other hand, is a more expansive network of individuals who act as independent advisers to you. Just as a company looks to its board for guidance, these people are there to offer you support in a broader sense. Each director usually specializes in a different area: a great manager, a skilled writer, a savvy freelancer, a wise parent, a compassionate friend, a talented peer, and so on. As such, each is able to offer you advice specific to their expertise.

The goal is to put together a group of people with experiences completely distinct from your own who can offer you a fresh perspective when needed. You can reach out to them with smaller asks than you would a mentor—though, over time, a few of them may grow into that role.

While there's no right or wrong way to build a board, here are a few tips I often suggest to my clients to help them start out on the right foot.

## Step 1: Understand Your Strengths, Gaps, and Aspirations

You can't enlist someone's help without knowing what you need from them first. To figure that out, you need to know what your strengths, weaknesses, and goals are. Begin by assessing where your career and personal life currently stand and how you want them to change (or not) in the future.

Ask yourself:

- What do I want my first job to look like? (if applicable)

- What do I like about my current role? What do I dislike?

- How can I do more of what I like and move away from what I don't?

- What do I enjoy outside of work? Are there hobbies I'm passionate about or new activities that I want to explore?

- What skills am I lacking right now? Do I know what to do to improve?

- How do I imagine my career path will look?

- Do I want a promotion? Do I want to make a lateral move or find a completely new role?

- How will I navigate my professional growth along with my personal goals, like starting a family or relocating?

These questions may vary depending on what stage of your career you're in. For instance, someone who is thinking about starting a family may be more focused on work-life balance, whereas a new grad may be more interested in defining their values and career interests. The big idea is to push yourself and dig deeper into what is important to you now, as well as in the next three to five years.

After jotting down your answers, use them to write a short letter (300 to 500 words) to your future self. Think about where you want to be three years from now, what you want to get better at, what you need to be more accountable for, and the areas in your work or your life where you could use some guidance.

Here's an example:

> Dear future self,
>
> I know that I'm a highly motivated, creative, collaborative, and determined person with a passion for helping others solve complex challenges. I know that I want to become a better data scientist and use my skills to create social impact, especially to tackle climate change. Three years from now, I hope to:
>
> • Be promoted to a managerial role and lead a motivated team underneath me
>
> • Learn data visualization skills to become better at my job as well as understand the skills required to manage a team
>
> • Expand my professional network by connecting with fellow data scientists and people working in the climate and energy sectors to learn from their experiences, gain regular feedback on my skills, and build new relationships
>
> • Prioritize my health by maintaining a regular four-day-a-week exercise routine and not compromising on my sleep as I do now
>
> • Set aside time to engage in volunteer work at least once a week, something I'm unable to get started on right now

Writing this note will help you figure out what your aspirations are and where you need to improve. It will also help you understand what kind of guidance you need and which individuals may be most useful to you as you create your board of directors. For instance, your interest in addressing climate change might push you to find other peers who are passionate about the energy sector and who can help you brainstorm ways to approach the problem. Your desire to build a healthy routine may encourage you to connect with people in different stages of their careers to learn about how they set work-life boundaries.

Finally, understand that your goals are not going to be static. They will evolve with your career, and as they do, you should reach out to new individuals for different perspectives.

## Step 2: Pick Your Board Members

Begin by looking around you. Are there people in your life whom you find inspiring? Depending on the advice you need, this could include a former peer, a friend's parent, a career coach, an alumnus of your college, or even your supervisor. Reach out to individuals from varied socioeconomic backgrounds, industries, roles, and organizations. Having people in various industries and life stages on your board will broaden your perspective, teach you new ways of doing things, and allow you to expand your network.

As you consider whom to include, ask yourself:

- Have I chosen a couple of people who already reached a goal that I have for myself or who have inspired me?

- Have I chosen people from diverse backgrounds?

- Have I chosen people who will challenge me to think and act critically? Have they been supportive of me and my goals in the past?

- Have I chosen people who will benefit from this relationship too?

I typically advise my clients to limit their board to three to six directors.

## Step 3: Reach Out to People

Your board can be as casual or as formal as you would like. Some people choose to simply treat their picks as board members without explicitly telling them, while others make more official requests.

If you choose to inform the people on your board, set up a call or an in-person meeting with them. Be direct, concise, and professional. Explain why you're reaching out, what you hope to get out of the relationship, and what you admire about or believe you can learn from them.

In your initial message, you could say:

Hey [name],

I'm reaching out because I've been building out a career board of directors—it's basically a group of people I really admire from whom I hope to learn as I grow in my career. You've been a great friend to me over the last five years, and I really value your guidance. Your passion for advocacy inspires me, and I would love to learn more about how to support the causes that resonate with you.

Would you be open to chatting with me on a call, or maybe over coffee? I'd love to include you in this group.

During your chat, have an honest conversation about what your expectations are and whether the potential board member can meet them. Do you want a monthly meeting? Would you prefer connecting over a call or in person? Try to stay flexible and be willing to adjust as the relationship progresses.

For instance, you might say, "My hope is that we'd be able to meet in person or hop on a call once a month to connect over the projects we're both working on. I'd love to share any useful insights with you and vice versa. I'd also be curious to learn more about the nonprofits you support and how best to advocate for the right causes."

If a prospective board member can't commit, that's OK—thank them for their time and ask if you can revisit the opportunity with them later on. You could say, "Thank you for being honest with me about your current commitments. Would you mind if we revisited this in a couple of months, when you may have more time?"

## Step 4: Give Back to Your Board

Managing a career board of directors requires a degree of time and effort. Remember, it's not just about you. Just as your board is helping you find fulfillment in your career, they should receive that same fulfillment by being a part of your journey. For instance, if you receive a promotion after a bunch of mock interviews with different directors on your board, take them out for a celebration, write them handwritten thank-you notes, or recognize them on LinkedIn.

There are so many meaningful ways to potentially engage with your directors. If a member of your board is looking to move out of their role into a new industry, for example, maybe you can give back by connecting them with someone you know. If one of them is looking for feedback on their kid's college application, step in and offer to help. If a member is looking to expand their network, introduce the different board members to one another. The stronger your rapport becomes with each director, the easier it will be for you to recognize ways you can contribute to their success and growth.

. . .

Deciding how to move forward in your career can be an isolating, anxiety-filled experience. You don't need to go it alone. Building a career board of directors is a great step toward taking ownership of your future, cultivating a valuable network of supporters, and, ultimately, finding fulfillment in your life and through your work.

## QUICK RECAP

When you're just getting started in your career, creating a personal board of directors can help you make decisions and move forward. Here's how to form one:

- Understand your strengths, weaknesses, and goals. Assess where your career stands and how you want it to change.

- Next, pick your board members. Reach out to individuals from varied socioeconomic backgrounds, industries, roles, and organizations who can help you achieve your goals.

- Finally, nurture your board with meaningful conversations and gestures. You can connect your directors with each other or offer to help if one of them is looking for guidance.

Adapted from content posted on hbr.org, May 9, 2022.

How do you build a network when you're just getting started in your career? Listen to this podcast:

# 7

# What to Say When You're Reaching Out to Someone on LinkedIn

by Kristi DePaul

If networking isn't at the top of your to-do list, it should be. Cultivating your network offers many benefits: greater learning opportunities, broader career prospects, access to leaders' insights, and more immediate job options, among others.[1] And there's no better place (at least online) to build your network than on LinkedIn.

LinkedIn offers the opportunity to track trends, make meaningful connections, and maintain a curated digital résumé that recruiters and potential employers can easily access and review. The problem is, while LinkedIn can help you build your network and career, few people are using it well—especially when it comes to reaching out to new contacts.

## Common Mistakes People Make While Networking on LinkedIn

If you've been hesitant to reach out to people on LinkedIn, or if you've been reaching out and not hearing back, there are strategies you can use to increase your chances. But first, let's look at five common mistakes you might be making:

- *You don't know what you want:* Have you thought about why you're reaching out to someone? Are you seeking more information about a role or company? A relationship that can grow? Or a lifeline to a potential future mentor or employer?

- *You're putting your own needs first:* Don't be self-serving. No one will respond to "It would be good to connect with you," unless they know what's in it for them.

- *Your messages are weak:* Generic, nonpersonalized messages have a low probability of success. As entrepreneur Larry Kim has said: "What are the 11 most boring words in the English language? *I'd like to add you to my professional network on LinkedIn.*"[2]

- *You're using an awkward tone:* Sometimes even the best messages will be met with silence or ghosting. Still, many continue to approach total strangers in ways they'd never dare in person.

- *You're not being persuasive enough:* If you haven't been able to convince the other person why you really want to connect with them, chances are they won't respond.

## Craft Messages That Get Responses

Now that you've identified what mistakes you may be making, let's look at how you can overcome them and flip the odds in your favor. No, there isn't a simple playbook or shortcut. But you can cut through the noise by employing research-backed approaches such as Cialdini's principles of persuasion and by borrowing proven practices from both regular folks and industry leaders.[3]

I reached out to experts, entrepreneurs, and authors who specialize in this area—from within my network and a few I wasn't connected to—to learn more about formulating messages that:

- Are authentic to you

- Will resonate with recipients at any level

Here's what they told me.

### If you are seeking advice on a career path or job change

People aren't employment oracles just waiting for your message soliciting their sage advice. Think deeply about the kind of guidance you want and then identify the most relevant person to approach.

"Clarity is key when you're performing cold outreach," Cynthia Johnson, author of *Platform: The Art and Science of Personal Branding*, told me. "Assume that the person you're reaching out to is busy and wants to give you the best advice possible. If you're direct and specific as to what you're asking and why you're asking them, you will have created the perfect environment for a confident and thoughtful response."

Sending a vague (and all-too-common) "Can I pick your brain?" message isn't going to be helpful. Tim Herrera, founding editor of Smarter Living at the *New York Times*, recommends being straightforward and transparent to improve your chances of receiving a reply. "Whatever the ask is, the best favor you can do for yourself is not to beat around the bush. You're teeing the recipient up to give you exactly what you want because they know exactly what that is. You've taken away the ambiguity for them, which will save them time and mental effort, and you're also setting up the exchange to be as productive and efficient as possible." Of course, he added, you should always aim to be kind and courteous.

Here's an example of a note that is precise, but is flexible on timing:

> Erica, your professional journey really stood out to me. I'm very interested in building my career as a [role]. Since you've been in that position, would you have some time to offer me a bit of advice on pursuing this? I would really appreciate a brief call at your convenience.

## If you want someone to review your résumé or cover letter

When making this kind of request, put yourself in the shoes of the receiver and try to answer this question for them up front: Why is this person contacting me? Acknowledge that you're asking them for a favor.

Here's a persuasive and considerate message that was sent my way:

> Hi Kristi, you've built a really interesting career in thought leadership, and [mutual contact] mentioned you were a great resource as she revised her résumé. Since I'm hoping to advance from [my current role], I'd love to get your brief take on my cover letter if your schedule allows it.

Receiving a carefully formulated request like this is somewhat rare, as it doesn't make any assumption that I can provide a labor-intensive line edit to someone's application materials. Again, the acknowledgment that I'm using my time to help matters. In cases where I've been referred to job seekers by other people I've helped, I'm even more likely to respond. If someone I help then pays it forward by assisting others in their own circles, that makes the investment worth it. (In other words: Always mention a referral if you have one.)

### If you are inquiring about a job posting and/or hiring process

"We all have demanding schedules and are a little burned out," explained Amber Naslund, principal content consultant at LinkedIn—a role she landed after building a consistent presence on the platform. "Open-ended messages like 'I just wondered if you had any openings . . .' aren't useful, because all of those details are on a company's career page and that puts the work on the person you're asking."

According to Naslund, it's better to ask about a specific role and see if someone is willing to introduce you to a recruiter, make an internal referral, or answer questions you have about that role, or the company. "Being respectful of people's time, expertise, and relationships can go a long way when you're trying to land your next job," she told me. The professional you reach out to could, for example, be a teammate who works closely with the role in question, or the person who would be the immediate supervisor.

You could try a message like this:

> Hi Cameron, I saw that your company is recruiting a marketing assistant. Since it seems you'd work directly with this person, it would be wonderful to hear your thoughts on the role. I'm looking to get some clarity on the role and responsibilities before I apply. Do you have a few minutes to speak with me about it in the next week or two?

## If you are approaching a potential mentor

Before sending an invitation to connect with a potential new mentor, investigate whether or not that person might be interested in serving as one.

Cynthia Johnson recommends looking for a leader who demonstrates that they (a) are experienced in the areas in which you're seeking mentorship and (b) show signs of having some availability.

Johnson found her longtime mentor on LinkedIn. "I assessed his expertise by doing diligent searches and thorough evaluations of his communications online with others." She identified the groups he had joined on the platform, including some where she noticed that he was very active, and joined them too. "His activity told me that he was interested in discussion and possibly had a bit of extra time to work with me," she said. "You can do this type of assessment, too, and find an amazing mentor."

When writing to a prospective mentor, make sure you've done your homework. Here's an example of a message you could send:

> Divya, your posts on edtech in the STEM education forum have been really thought provoking! I've interned for a few startups in this space and am excited about my own next steps—but I definitely could use some guidance from an experienced pro like you. Would you be open to chatting about this?

## If you are reaching out for help after a recent job loss

Contextualizing your messages will make all the difference. If you're searching for help finding a job, strike up a conversation about your experience, what you're looking for, and who you feel might be helpful, Amber Naslund said. "It's a great way to warm up the conversation and increase the likelihood that a new connection is willing to make some helpful introductions. People's networks are sacrosanct; most of us have worked very hard over a number of years to gain the trust of our networks and the people we've worked with, so we're not likely to open that up to just anyone and make cold introductions."

Here's an example of what you could say to let the other person know why you're reaching out to them:

> Eitan, I'm looking to join a mission-driven team like yours and just happened to see your colleague's post about the product manager role. Would you be the right person to ask about one of the technical requirements? Let me know if I could send an email your way.

. . .

According to an old Chinese proverb, the best time to plant a tree was 20 years ago; the second-best time is now. So if you haven't cultivated your network, it's time to get started. It's understandable that reaching out to people you've never met might feel intimidating—and that it means facing possible rejection. Try to remember that not only is rejection normal, but it also indicates you're aiming high enough to achieve even greater success. Growth of any kind involves some risk. The advantage: You'll learn valuable lessons and can continually improve along the way.

## QUICK RECAP

Networking online, and especially on LinkedIn, can be challenging. But there are ways to make your messages to potential connections stand out:

- If you're not getting messages back, consider what might not be working with your approach. Are you unsure about what you really want?

- Be clear about your intentions in reaching out, avoid vague lines such as "Can I pick your brain?," and mention personal referrals when you have them.

- Do your own research before reaching out to someone. If job postings at a company are easily found online, for example, don't ask someone if there are any openings.

---

Adapted from content posted on hbr.org,
November 2, 2020.

How can you optimize your presence on LinkedIn?
Watch this video:

# 8

# Five Questions to Ask During an Informational Interview

by Sean O'Keefe

What career is right for me?

Answering this question can be a confusing and exhausting process. Where do you begin and to whom do you go for advice?

Sometimes, you may think you've found the perfect job but wonder if the description online accurately describes what you'll do in the role. Or you may be considering many different options at once and feeling unsure about which to pursue. What questions should you be asking to help you make an informed decision?

Setting up time to chat with someone working in the position or at the company you're considering is a great way to get an inside perspective into what that career entails. These chats are often called informational interviews, or, as I like to call them, career conversations.

Career conversations are a means to informally learn about roles, organizations, and industries. They're also a strategic way to develop internal advocates, provide you with knowledge needed to land positions you are seeking, and be referred into formal interview processes.

## Land the Conversation

The first step to conducting a successful career conversation is to get a professional to say yes to your outreach request. Make a list of the organizations you want to work for, then research professionals at those companies who are about five to 10 years further into their careers and may be in a position to make entry-level hires.

Successful outreach messages are short and polite. Give a sentence of context about who you are, mention why this specific person could be helpful to you, and be flexible in scheduling. For example:

> "Hi [name]. I'm a final-year student at [university] and I'm exploring my career options in organizational strategy. I am reaching out to you to request a short conversation so I can learn more about your role and how you got here. Your experience and advice would really help me make more informed choices as I start my career. I'm happy to speak at a time convenient to you."

Most important, I suggest that you send a follow-up message about two days later, then another three days after that if you still don't get a response. Persistence is key. If you still don't hear from the person, look for your next best alternative.

Once you've set up time to chat, you need to prepare. Write down a set of questions in order of priority, then adjust as needed during the conversation. It's OK to go off-script too; these questions are there to guide your conversation. Remember that you're there to learn as much as you can and build a relationship, which are more important than getting through your prepared questions.

## Set the Stage

Once you land the virtual or in-person meeting, kick things off with some small talk. Start with a few simple, open-ended questions before asking about their career. Your conversation should be driven by genuine human connection—it shouldn't feel like an investigative interview.

Thank the other person for taking the time to chat with you. Then, in the first minute or two, you might ask how their day is going, where they are located (a great conversation starter for video calls), or what they are currently working on.

Next, give a short overview of who you are and why you are interested in speaking with them. Touch on the highlights of your education and your work and/or internships and be open about any current decisions or uncertainty you're facing. This will give the other person context so that they get to know you a bit better and can be most helpful to you.

# Get Your Answers

Now it's time to get the answers you are looking for.

The five questions below are designed to help you get an inside view into the company or career you are interested in, as well as connect on a human level with the person you're speaking with.

**1. Could you walk me through your career path, starting with your experiences at [name of college they attended] and any internships or jobs you had before your role as [name of current position]?**

This question will push the other person to share the most relevant details of their career path and how they ended up in their current job. It also shows that you did some research about their background and education. Asking this question gives you a view into the key decisions and stepping stones that propelled them to where they are today (and how you can get there, too).

**Potential follow-up question:** What did it take to move from one position to another?

**2. I understand you [share what you know about their job duties]. Can you provide more details about what your typical day/week looks like?**

If you're interested in learning more about the daily rhythms and routines of this person's work, this question can help to demystify their job responsibilities and tasks. As the person is answering, ask yourself whether you could imagine yourself waking up every day and happily doing the work they are describing. Would you find the best parts of the role inspiring? The toughest parts tolerable?

**Potential follow-up question:** What part of your job do you find the most interesting, as well as the most challenging?

### 3. Which skills are most important for a job like yours?

Understanding what skills are required for their job is key, actionable information. It gives you a roadmap of which capabilities you might need to learn or improve upon should you pursue a similar role. Keep in mind that this answer will likely vary depending on the role and tenure of the person. Employees at the bottom of the hierarchy are likely to use more technical and detail-oriented skills to get the job done, while more senior employees likely spend more time managing, developing, and leading others.

**Potential follow-up question:** Are there any additional skills that you think will be especially useful in the next five years for a student like me entering the field?

### 4. What do you think is the best way to earn an internship (or job) in this industry (or at this company)?

A professional who does (or has done) the job you are considering applying to will be able to give much more concrete and useful advice than any article you read. Companies' websites are sometimes vague about what they look for in applicants, so asking a hiring manager or current employee is likely to yield more actionable insights. You might also learn about skills or experiences that you can invest in to raise your odds of getting hired in your desired field.

**Potential follow-up question:** Is not knowing [skill name] a deal-breaker?

**5. I'm really interested in speaking with people [in X field/ in Y role/at Z company]. Who else would you recommend that I connect with?**

This question is valuable because it opens the possibility for you to engage in additional career conversations that can increase your social capital and broaden your opportunities to earn positions in the hidden job market (positions that are not advertised online). Based on your interests, you can ask about other employees at the same company, professionals in a specific field, or people with a similar set of life experiences who share some of your interests. This question should be asked toward the end of the conversation.

**Potential follow-up question:** Would you mind making an introduction to [person's name]?

. . .

Don't be afraid to stray from this list. You bring your personal experience and goals into the conversation, so ask questions that you are truly curious about relating to the other person's career. You will likely be surprised and excited by how gracious and helpful people can be—even highly successful and busy professionals.

## QUICK RECAP

Having an informational interview can be a great way to gain insight about a specific career path, role, or individual's experience. Here's how to approach one:

- Create a list of people you'd like to learn from and reach out with a short message. Once you get a yes, prepare a set of questions to make the most of the conversation.

- Start with some open-ended questions before asking about their career. Then ask questions to get an inside view into how the person got their role and what skills you should be working on.

- Your conversation should be driven by genuine human connection—it should not feel like an investigative interview.

Adapted from content posted on hbr.org, October 1, 2021.

# 9

# Are You Taking Full Advantage of Your Network?

by Deborah Grayson Riegel

Our networks can serve many different purposes—they can help us understand our goals, land jobs, and explore new career opportunities.

But for me, networking is more than just a means to an end. I like to think about my network as serving three core purposes:

1. *My network provides me with insights, experiences, and perspectives that expand my own knowledge and thinking.* This makes me a valuable resource to my colleagues and clients.

2. *My network allows me to help others.* While many of us think of our networks as people who can help *us*, we need to remember that those relationships are a give-and-take. I've got plenty of energy, inspiration, connections, resources, and support to give.

3. *My network helps sharpen my communication skills.* Having
   a broad and diverse network gives me the chance to
   practice the very skills that I help others develop as a part
   of my coaching and training work. From communicating
   in virtual environments to navigating tricky conversations, my network is the perfect laboratory to practice
   within.

You can similarly leverage the power of your network to make
gains beyond landing a job. Here's how.

# 1. Use Your Network to Learn

Networks are among the primary knowledge conduits of the
world. Throughout our lives, we learn from people that we know.
The spread of knowledge through a network resembles the spread
of infection. In other words, learning is contagious.[1]

All of us can benefit from catching the wisdom, knowledge,
and experience that our networks provide. There's actually a term
for this: network intelligence.

This kind of learning doesn't just come from the people
we interact with most often. Interestingly, we are most likely to
learn from our dormant ties, or former colleagues, peers, and
friends with whom we've lost touch.[2] Because we're not constantly engaging with these people, they have much to offer us.
While we're off living our lives, growing and learning, they're
doing the same. Reconnecting allows us to exchange that information, share knowledge, and introduce each other to skills we
can leverage.

## How to network with the goal of learning

- *Build your network to supplement your knowledge of different industries and areas of expertise.* Strive to connect with people with diverse backgrounds and educations; people of different genders, races, sexualities, and abilities; and people from different geographies, cultures, fields, and sectors.

- *Think about what you know, and more specifically, what you know how to do.* Offer your expertise to the people who may want to learn from you in exchange for their advice and expertise. You should also consider your "beyond the job" knowledge. For instance, I'm not a travel agent, but my connections often tap me to help them plan trips since I'm well traveled. Similarly, I have a connection who got certified in mindfulness practices on the side of her day job, and I can call her when I need a little emotional support.

- *Reengage weak ties.* Send an email to a former colleague, peer, professor, or a friend with whom you've lost touch. It doesn't have to be complicated or apologetic. You can say something like, "Hi there! I've been thinking about you and realized it's been a few years since we last connected. I would love to catch up at a time that works for you. Are you game? And if so, do you prefer phone, Zoom, or a cup of coffee?" Follow up once or twice—and if you don't hear back, try again in a few months.

## 2. Use Your Network to Help Others

Humans are prosocial creatures, meaning we are wired to help other people. Helping others can give us a helper's high—similar to a runner's high—where we release endorphins that make us feel good. Helping others also triggers our reciprocity bias. When we help someone out, they are more likely to help us out in return.

So much of networking feels like asking for things, so offering your knowledge, skills, advice, or expertise is a way to differentiate yourself and build deeper connections with people who may help grow your career down the line.

### How to network with the goal of helping

- *Develop your help fluency—a range of ways you can be helpful to your network beyond just making connections.* Think about what you're good at, what you like to do, and what others often ask for your help with. This can range from listening empathetically and giving pep talks to helping someone celebrate a big win. You can help your network battle loneliness simply by reaching out.

- *Identify some low-hanging-fruit opportunities to help people in your network.* These are activities that, for you, are easy, rewarding, satisfying, and require little time. For example, if you're a great editor, and you can do it easily and quickly, offer to proofread the résumé and cover

letter of a contact who is getting ready to go on the
job market.

- *Play the long game.*[3] Think about your long-term career
  goals (one to three years from now) and identify people in
  your network who may be able to help you down the
  road. Now is the time to offer them help. For instance,
  perhaps you have a friend from college who is working in
  an industry you want to explore in the future. Reach out
  to them to reconnect, check in, and ask what they might
  be looking for help with. It could be access to a professional connection, to leverage a skill that you have, or
  even something more personal, like a recommendation
  for an accountant. You won't know until you put
  yourself out there. Don't think of it as a quid pro quo.
  Consider it an investment in your future relationship
  that may pay off.

## 3. Use Your Network to Sharpen Your Communication Skills

Many of us hate talking to strangers, but doing so gives us an
opportunity to practice our conversation skills. Networking
requires us to listen to others—their needs, values, pain points,
interests, and hopes. Yet, we are notoriously bad at it. According
to research from the University of California, those of us who
haven't worked specifically to develop our listening skills understand and retain only about 50% of any conversation. Forty-eight
hours later, that rate drops to less than 25%.[4]

That's why it's so important to practice. Networking allows us to sharpen skills that will help us in every other part of our careers: curiosity, persuasion, confidence, and executive presence, as well as learning how to speak engagingly and keep the attention of an audience.

These are skills that make us better problem-solvers, decision-makers, speakers, presenters, and communicators. They teach us how to ask smart questions and share our ideas without oversharing or dominating conversations.

## How to network with the goal of sharpening your communication skills

- Identify one or two communication skills you'd like to improve (such as listening without interrupting or describing what you do succinctly) and practice those skills during an upcoming networking conversation. If you're feeling particularly bold, ask your new connection for feedback!

- Have a conversation with someone in your network that you know holds different political, social, religious, or other views from your own. Practice having a respectful dialogue and exchange of ideas. Lead the conversation with curiosity.

- Practice your pitching skills by suggesting that your new connection meet with someone in your current network. Tell a compelling story about how you met this other person, articulate why you think they'd be a good resource for your new connection, and ask if you can make an introduction. Then write a clear, concise, and compelling email introducing these two people.

. . .

Networking shouldn't just be about what you need right now. It should be about learning, helping others, and growing yourself in the process. Don't sell yourself short—leverage your network for all it's worth.

## QUICK RECAP

Networking is more than just a means to an end. Here are three ways to leverage your network and grow your career:

- **Exchange expertise.** Don't be afraid to reach out to your dormant ties—reconnecting will allow you to exchange information, share knowledge, and learn new skills.

- **Help others.** When we help someone out, they are more likely to help us out in return. Think about your long-term career goals and identify people in your network who may be able to help you down the road.

- **Sharpen your communication skills.** Identify one or two communication skills you'd like to improve (such as listening without interrupting) and practice them during an upcoming networking conversation.

Adapted from content posted on hbr.org, November 28, 2022.

Wondering how you can use a platform like Instagram
to network? Watch this video:

# 10

# How to Talk to Your Boss About Your Career Development

## by Antoinette Oglethorpe

Some people enter the workforce thinking their manager is responsible for their career development. They work hard, deliver results, sit back, and wait to be promoted.

Unfortunately, this strategy rarely works.

The truth is: Your career development starts with you—and is amplified by the support of your manager. To advance in any role, you need to proactively initiate a career-planning conversation with your boss. This is a meeting you can use to discuss your interest in growth opportunities, ensure that your individual goals are aligned with the mission of the organization, and develop a longer-term plan to set you up for success.

If this sounds like a lot of work to you—your assumption is correct. Career conversations take significant planning and preparation, but in the end, you will walk away with a better idea of how to advance. Here is a step-by-step guide to help you get pro-active about your growth and set up a productive career conversation with your boss.

# Ahead of the Meeting

### Start by reflecting on what you want

Before approaching your boss, you need to have a clear understanding of where you are right now and where you want to be in a few years. This will help you verbalize your professional goals and create a development plan in service of them. Set aside some time in your busy schedule to reflect on your present status and your future goals. Ask yourself the following questions:

**Where are you now?** Think about the tasks you do on a daily basis as well as any projects or priorities on your plate. Which aspects of this work do you find energizing versus draining? Which areas do you consistently feel confident in and which do you consistently struggle with?

Take stock of whether you have mastered the skills needed to succeed at your current level. Gaining this clarity will allow you to more intentionally seek out opportunities where you can leverage your strengths and also identify stretch projects you can use for growth and improvement.

Also seek feedback from peers. Does your analysis of your strengths and weaknesses match theirs? What, in their eyes, sets you apart from others?

**What's important to you in the long term?** The goal of this question is to help you identify your values and how they fit into your work. You need to understand this to create a development plan that will help you build a fulfilling career.

Think about what you want to do next. In two years, what kind of role do you see yourself in? When you imagine this dream job, what are you willing to compromise on and what is nonnegotiable?

Recall the tasks that you found most energizing. For example, you might realize that administrative tasks drain you and interacting with clients energizes you. How does this fit into your image of the future? How does it fit into your next role at your current organization? Perhaps being promoted into a role that includes more face time with clients is a nonnegotiable, whereas administrative work is something you will need to negotiate or compromise on. This information will be valuable during your career conversation with your boss.

Before moving on, as a last consideration, think about how your ambitions align with the mission or goals of your team and organization. If you can connect your future goals back to the goals of the company, you can present your manager with a more convincing argument for your growth.

**What does success look like to you?** Success means different things to different people—an upward trajectory is just one version. Maybe, upon reflecting, you've realized that you don't want to take on more responsibility or become a people manager. Maybe, to you, success involves more work-life balance and heads-down creative work. Define your version of success so that your manager understands your ambitions and can help you reach them.

## Request a meeting with your manager

A career conversation should not be folded into your weekly one-on-one meeting with your manager or tagged onto your performance review. It should be a separate meeting specifically focused on discussing career growth. The frequency of career conversations will vary, but ideally, your manager should be open to holding them several times a year to allow for ongoing feedback, goal setting and alignment, and the discussion of new or upcoming career development opportunities. It's usually best to have them shortly after an annual or semiannual performance review—when you've already spent time reflecting on your past work—and can now develop a forward-looking plan.

When requesting a career conversation, be clear about the purpose of the meeting. You want your manager to have time to prepare. Send them an email along the lines of:

> Hi [name],
>
> I wanted to find some time on your calendar to meet and discuss my career development. I have been at the company for a little over a year now and think this conversation could help me understand how I can grow professionally and contribute more to the success of our team and larger organization.
>
> Can I set an hour aside for us to discuss this next week?

# During the Meeting

## Start on a positive note

Begin the conversation by expressing gratitude for the opportunity. You could say, "Thank you so much for meeting with me today—I really appreciate it. I'd like to use this time to discuss my career aspirations, and hopefully come up with a development plan that will help me align my goals with our larger team goals and the goals of the company."

Next, clearly articulate the insights you discovered during your self-reflection time. Explain where you see yourself currently, including the aspects of your role that feel fulfilling and those you would like to grow in, change, or develop in new ways. For instance, you might say, "I feel most fulfilled when I'm working with clients and think that my welcoming and clear communication style is a strength that sets me apart on the team."

Move on to recapping your achievements and highlight how they have contributed to the success of your team or company. This will not only demonstrate your value, but it will also provide a foundation for the conversation around your growth. You could say, "Over the past year, I successfully led the X project, which resulted in a $x\%$ increase in client engagement—contributing to the organizational goal of increasing client engagement by $y\%$. I believe this shows my potential to take on more challenging client-facing roles on our team and coach others on how to successfully do the same."

Follow up by sharing what's important to you in the next stage of your career and how you see those changes contributing to your long-term growth: "As I grow at the company, I'd love to continue taking on more client-facing projects, and eventually, leading them. I see this as a way to further develop my communication skills and grow as a people leader, which is a role I want to grow into."

Finally, if there are development areas you want to acknowledge, don't ignore them. Instead, connect them back to the vision of the organization. You could add, "I know I still have more to learn about project management, and taking on more initiatives will allow me to do this. The company wants to increase our client outreach this year, so my growth would help contribute to that goal." Remember, your career goals should create a win-win situation for both you and the organization.

## Identify next steps

You've just given your manager a lot to think about, and it may take them some time to formulate a response. After making your case, follow up with something like, "I'm curious to hear your thoughts and feedback."

In some cases, your manager may thank you for opening up the discussion and ask to revisit the conversation in a week—giving them more time to process and come up with a plan. In the best-case scenario, your manager will have come more prepared, with their own idea about where they can see you growing. In this case, you can work together to develop next steps.

Start by discussing the following areas:

- *Understanding the opportunities available to you.* Ask your manager what opportunities are available to you given your goals and aspirations. Do you need to learn new skills before moving up the ladder? If so, what are they and how can you better demonstrate them? Do they feel you are ready to take on a stretch project? If there are no opportunities on your team, is there another team you could work with in order to grow?

- *Navigating the processes and politics of the organization.* Your manager is not the sole decision-maker in most cases, especially when it comes to promotions. You need to understand how the organization works, including both processes and tactics, who the key influencers are, and how to raise your profile and be more visible to key people. Ask your boss, "Are there other people in the organization whose work I should be observing more closely? I would love to speak with them and learn how they've become successful here. How would you suggest I make my work and myself more visible?"

- *Identifying and evaluating different options and opportunities.* It's unlikely that you and your manager will put together an elaborate plan in this very first meeting. Once your manager presents you with options, thank them for their insights. Then, let them know that you will think about what you discussed. Ask if you can take some time to outline a more tangible plan for them to review in a follow-up meeting. This will give you the space you need to reflect on the pros and cons of your discussion and propose a few solid next steps.

# After the Meeting

## Draft a development plan

Take what you've learned and put together a forward-looking plan that outlines next steps, including any new skills you need to acquire, any projects you've agreed to take on, and any important stakeholders you want to begin building relationships with. Remember, the best plans are both ambitious and realistic, pushing your boundaries while still being achievable. Use SMART (Specific, Measurable, Achievable, Relevant, Time-bound) goals so you can monitor your progress over time. While there will always be factors that are out of your control, it's useful to structure your plan using concrete milestones (even if they are subject to change). For instance, setting a goal like "finishing the leadership training program within six months" or "increasing client engagement by 10% in Q2" are more feasible than something unpredictable like "be promoted to people leader by fall of 2024."

## Follow up

Once you've outlined your goals and milestones, set up some time to review your plan with your manager. Try to do this no later than a week after the first meeting so that the conversation is still top of mind. It can be helpful to send your manager your plan prior to your discussion to give them time to review it thoughtfully beforehand.

Use your follow-up meeting to gather their feedback, make adjustments, and ensure that you're both aligned. Then ask if you can check in on how things are progressing—either in additional follow-up meetings or during your regular check-ins throughout the year.

. . .

Career conversations are vital to your professional growth. By initiating them, you make your ambitions known, gain valuable feedback, and pave the way for a fulfilling career path. Prepare well, communicate clearly, and always be open to feedback. In doing so, you'll empower yourself to move forward, secure the knowledge you need to grow, and give your manager an opportunity to fully understand and support you on your journey.

## QUICK RECAP

To advance in any role, you need to proactively initiate a career-planning conversation with your boss. Here's how:

- Reflect on where you are right now and where you want to be in a few years. What do you find energizing versus draining? What kind of role do you see yourself in?

- Request a meeting with your manager, during which you share your goals and achievements.

- After the meeting, draft a plan that outlines next steps, including any new skills you need to acquire, any projects you've agreed to take on, and any important stakeholders you want to begin building relationships with.

---

Adapted from content posted on hbr.org, August 1, 2023.

# How Do I Decide What's Next?

# How to Make Better Decisions About Your Career

by Timothy Yen

Choosing the perfect career, considering grad school, deciding to leave your job and move to a new one—decisions like these can feel daunting. We all spend a huge amount of time at work, and we all want (and deserve) to love what we do. But the path to finding that work isn't always clear.

Luckily, there are actions you can take to help you figure out what's right for you. Use this five-step framework to narrow down your options and focus on what's important.

**Editor's note:** This framework was adapted from *Choose Better: The Optimal Decision-Making Framework*, by Timothy Yen.

## 1. What Are Your Feelings Telling You?

If you want to find a fulfilling career, it needs to align with your values. Your feelings can help you discern this, even if you haven't consciously named what those values are.

Think of it this way: When you're faced with an important decision, what's the first thing that happens in your mind and your body? Usually, before logic kicks in, you'll experience a strong emotion. Pay attention to that. Your emotions are connected to who you are at your core and can provide important insights about your identity and the values that may be driving your actions but that are also, at times, beyond your conscious awareness.

So, think about the kind of work you're doing now, or the kind of work you'd like to do. What feelings come up? If you feel anger, sadness, or even fear and anxiety when thinking about your options, consider those feelings red flags. If, on the other hand, you feel happiness or excitement, that's an indicator that what you're considering might be a good decision.

If you don't feel like any of your options elicit positive emotions, go back to the drawing board. Consider different possibilities until you find something that is in alignment with your emotions.

## 2. What Matters to You?

Once you've connected with your emotions, you're ready for the next step: consciously identifying your values. Your values can be defined as what really matters to you, or your why. That is, they can help you define why a certain decision feels more meaningful to you than another. Understanding your why will allow you to make choices that align directly with the things you care about—choices that will keep you fulfilled longer term.

For example, let's say you're trying to decide between two jobs that you've been offered. One is a high-paying corporate job and the other is a job working at a nonprofit with a reasonable, but lower, salary. If you take the time to identify your values and find that helping others is one of them, but money isn't high on your list, that makes your decision to work at the nonprofit a bit easier.

There are a number of ways to figure out what your values are. One of the best is through formal psychological assessments. My favorite is the Enneagram personality test because the results describe your personality traits and motivations in the context of ideal circumstances *and* stressful situations, which can give you a more holistic look at who you are.[1] But there are a number of other credible resources out there as well: DISC, LIFO Survey, Big Five Personality Test, 16 Personality Factors Test, and Hogan's Motive, Values, Preference Inventory (MVPI).[2] All of these tests are supported by science and extensive research.

If you don't want to take a formal assessment, there are a few other options. The Passion Test, by Janet and Chris Atwood, asks you a series of questions and has you rank your interests from most important to least important.[3] Examples of these questions include "What subject could I read 500 books or watch countless videos about without getting bored?" and "What would I spend my time doing if I had complete financial abundance to do anything?" It may seem straightforward, but recalling your interests in a direct and honest way can help you name values that previously seemed elusive.

## 3. What Matters to the People in Your Life?

None of us exists in a vacuum. Just as it's important to get clear on what matters to you, it's also important to consider how any decision you make will impact your loved ones—because it probably will.

Whether it's a partner, family member, or friend, ask the people who will be affected by your choices for their own thoughts, input, and feelings. This is especially important if you're making a decision about your career. Often, these kinds of choices have a strong influence over your finances and living situation, as well as the amount of time you can dedicate to certain relationships.

For example, let's say you're offered a job that you're excited about that aligns with your values, but it requires you to commute two hours into work every day. You may be OK with this personally, but you must acknowledge that this is time you will lose out on spending with your significant other, family, or friends. Your decision, then, not only impacts you—it impacts those you care about.

This doesn't necessarily mean that you shouldn't take the job. However, it might mean that you should take the time to negotiate the offer to make it more closely aligned with both your values and those of the people around you. In this case, you might ask the hiring manager for a flexible work arrangement, one in which you come into the office only three days a week to limit your commute.

# 4. What Is the Reality of the Situation?

The goal of asking yourself this question is to make sure that you are making your choices for the right reasons. You want to ensure that the decision you are about to make is based on correct data, not an erroneous interpretation of your situation. Otherwise, you might end up having false expectations or feeling disappointed by the choice you make.

To answer this question, you have to be objective and consider the realities surrounding your options, not your assumptions. For example, let's say you're thinking about quitting your job because you think your coworkers aren't friendly. Before you make the big decision to leave your organization, ask, "Do I have information to back up my logic or am I making an assumption?" Maybe your coworkers seem unfriendly but are actually just shy. Maybe they're too focused on work to socialize. Or, maybe you're right, and they really are unfriendly. You won't know for sure unless you step back and look at the situation objectively.

Write down a description of the experiences you've had that back up your logic, but don't include any interpretations. Just describe what happened. Taking time to pause and describe creates an opportunity for you to evaluate things more clearly—and you can apply this tactic to any kind of situation.

If you're still in doubt about whether you've come to the correct conclusion after you've done this, double-check your conclusions with someone you trust, such as a friend or counselor.

## 5. How Do You Put the Pieces Together?

Once you've answered these four questions, you've laid the foundation for making an optimal decision. But there's still one last step: putting all the pieces together.

How do you do that?

Start by reviewing all the information you've just discovered. For example, if you are trying to decide on a career path, consider the emotions you felt as you looked at your potential job choices. Ask yourself, "How do I feel and why do I feel this way?"

Next, review your values. Do the job choices that excite you align with those values? What about the values of your loved ones? This should help narrow down your list.

Finally, give yourself a reality check. Are there any factors driving your decision that are based on assumptions rather than information?

It will take time, but giving your full attention to each of these points should help you reach a rational, appropriate decision about what career path is best for you, no matter what your current situation is. Not only that, but you'll also know, on a deeper level, that the decision you're making is in full alignment with your values, your emotions, yourself, and the people you love. And when it comes to a major decision like finding your perfect career, that's exactly as it should be.

## QUICK RECAP

Making decisions is hard—especially when it comes to your career. These questions can help you focus on what's important:

- **What are your feelings telling you?** If you feel anger, sadness, or even fear and anxiety when thinking about your options, consider those feelings red flags.

- **What matters to you?** Understanding your values will allow you to make choices that align directly with the things you care about.

- **What matters to the people in your life?** It's important to consider how your decision will impact your loved ones. Ask them for their own thoughts, input, and feelings.

- **What is the reality of the situation?** Be objective and consider the realities surrounding your options, not your assumptions.

- **How do you put the pieces together?** Review all of the information you've gathered and continue running through these questions until you reach your decision.

Adapted from content posted on
hbr.org, May 19, 2021.

Are you weighing the trade-offs of a big career decision? Listen to this podcast:

# The Right Way to Make a Big Career Transition

by Utkarsh Amitabh

When Amazon founder Jeff Bezos was deciding when to quit his well-paying hedge fund job, he went to his boss and told him that he was thinking of selling books online. He had already been talking to him about the power of the internet, but for the first time he was seriously considering quitting to become an entrepreneur. His boss was startled to hear that someone would actually leave a coveted investing job to work on something with so many unknowns. After all, aren't good investors experts in evaluating risk?

His boss decided to take him out for a two-hour walk in Central Park in New York City. He wanted to understand what was going on in Bezos's mind. During the walk, Bezos managed to convince him that selling books online had great potential and e-commerce could be really big. His boss agreed it was a good idea but said that it would be a better idea for somebody who didn't already have a good job. Bezos was given 48 hours to make a final decision.

To figure out the next steps in his career, Bezos came up with the regret minimization framework, a simple mental model to minimize the number of regrets in the long run.[1] He asked himself what he would regret more when he was 80 years old: trying to build something he had strong conviction in and failing, or failing to give it a try? He realized that not trying would haunt him every day.

When he thought about his career transition, keeping the regret minimization framework in mind, quitting turned out to be an incredibly easy decision. He left the hedge fund in the middle of the year and walked away from his massive annual bonus.

Whether you are pursuing a passion or a side hustle, confused about quitting your job for a new one, or just looking for a change, know that it's not a straightforward decision. It requires careful planning and thinking. I can say that with some conviction because I've had to make this tricky decision myself. In the middle of the pandemic, I quit my job at Microsoft to work full-time on my passion project. I loved my work, but the more I reflected on my core values, the kind of life I wanted to build, and the way I wanted to use my skills, the more it became clear to me that entrepreneurship was the way forward.

I had nurtured my passion project as a side hustle for four years: Network Capital, a global peer-to-peer networking community of 100,000-plus ambitious and curious millennials. There were so many questions running through my head during this time. Why should I quit to make this my full-time job? Is this what I really want? When should I quit? Poet Mary Oliver's words kept ringing in my head: "What is it you plan to do with your one wild and precious life?"

Most important, I wondered if I would regret not giving it a shot. But making that decision turned out to be more complex than I had thought.

Transitions aren't just about doing something different. A career transition is a lifestyle redesign that often entails rethinking how you want to feel at the end of the day, how you want to spend your time, and how this relates to your longer-term goals. When you feel this need for change, it isn't necessarily related to a fancier title or more money, but your inner voice whispering that you could do more, be more, experience and achieve more.

If you're thinking about quitting your job to make a meaningful career transition, first think about the why, the what, and the when.

## Why (Do You Want to Change)?

### Start by asking why you want to quit your current job

Is it the culture of the organization, is it the people you work with, or is there something else bogging you down? Like me, you might also discover that you love your job, but you want to build something new or experiment with a different sector. It is critical to be radically honest with yourself and think things through.

I decided to conduct an experiment to figure out my career transition. For the past four years, I'd worked on building Network Capital on nights and over weekends. I decided to take two weeks off from work to focus solely on this task. That is when I realized that I could make so much more progress on my side hustle with focused effort. It made me realize that I enjoyed dedicating most of my waking hours to my side hustle, even though I loved my day job.

> **PRO TIP:** Before leaving your job, try to find ways to experience what your next position might feel like. Does it feel better than what you are doing now? Is it worth committing to this change? If you are able, take some time off from work—even just a week—to focus on your passion project. If you don't have a passion project and are just looking for something new, use your free time (weekends or after hours) to experiment with the industries or roles you are interested in. This might mean volunteering, job shadowing, or even conducting informational interviews with people who have careers you admire.

## Keep the end in mind

It is challenging to plan for the long-term, but it helps to have a mental image of the kind of life you want to build.

Work and life are not separate entities. Work is part of life. Try to visualize where you want to live, the kind of person you want to partner with (or if you even want a partner), and how you want to spend your time on a daily basis.

I knew I wanted autonomy over a strict daily schedule. I wanted geographical flexibility because of my desire to help young people navigate their careers around the world. I wanted to create a job that gave my future self a deeper sense of purpose.

While I could have indirectly made an impact in the career navigation space at Microsoft, I knew I wanted a more direct connection with the people I was trying to serve. Committing to Network Capital full-time would give me that opportunity.

> **PRO TIP:** Write your future autobiography. Before leaving Microsoft, I actually sat down and wrote a sort-of autobiography. I reflected on what the most defining events along the way would be. I was intentional about describing (in great detail) what I wanted to be remembered for and the way I spent my time. Eventually, how you spend your time is who you become. Conducting this thought experiment gave me more clarity on what mattered most to me and why. This doesn't need to be 100 pages long, but it does need to give you an idea of what you want your journey to be.

## What (Do You Want to Do)?

### Assess yourself

While some may already know they want to work in another industry or go back to school to learn something new, many don't know what their next step should be. But it is impossible to know where you are going if you don't know where you are. The simplest way to conduct this self-assessment is to ask yourself these questions:

- What's my end goal?

- If I keep doing what I am doing today, will I get closer to my ultimate goal?

- Will my 80-year-old self have more or fewer regrets because of my current choices?

After that, write down the steps you will need to take to make your future self proud and the problems that you might encounter in doing that. An important part of learning where you are is in understanding the challenges that are keeping you there. Then, look at the list of things you need to do to get closer to your goal. Find, know, or strike out challenges you have no control over.

For me, one issue that I couldn't control—at least in the short term—was income predictability. Would I make an equal amount of money at Network Capital as I did at Microsoft? Would I need to change my lifestyle? In general, corporate compensation is significantly higher (at least in the early days) than the income one can expect in early-stage ventures. Complaining about it or worrying about it obsessively would have been a waste of time. If quitting got me closer to my goal, and I chose to pursue that goal, how would I work around this problem?

I came up with a plan inspired by *Wired* cofounder Kevin Kelley's concept of 1,000 True Fans. Kelley advises:

> 1,000 True Fans is an alternative path to success other than stardom. Instead of trying to reach the narrow and unlikely peaks of platinum bestseller hits, blockbusters, and celebrity status, you can aim for direct connection with a thousand true fans. On your way, no matter how

many fans you actually succeed in gaining, you'll be surrounded not by faddish infatuation, but by genuine and true appreciation. It's a much saner destiny to hope for. And you are much more likely to actually arrive there.[2]

I gave myself the target of getting Network Capital 1,000 monthly paying subscribers over a period of 12 months. I built a strategy around how I would bring in money, gave my goals a real structure, and was able to increase our number of loyal, engaged subscribers over time.

> **PRO TIP:** Approach your self-assessment with aware-ness, curiosity, and a willingness to experiment. Author and entrepreneur Marie Forleo says, "Everything is figureoutable."[3] When it comes to career transitions, there isn't a formula per se. Experimenting, tinkering, and figuring things out is the way forward.

## When (Will the Change Happen)?

### Expect multiple rejections

Unfortunately, most career transitions and hiring processes rely heavily on past experience. For example, suppose you are a technology sales manager who wants to break into trading or hedge funds. Most recruiters will nudge you toward a role very similar to your current job, even if you have the skills necessary to transition to a different sector.

Even at Microsoft, when I was looking to transition from corporate strategy to business development, it turned out to be much more challenging than I had thought. After approaching peers on dozens of teams, I realized that very few wanted to take a bet on someone with a different experience. Finally, one hiring manager gave me a project to work on. I performed well on that project and got the opportunity to interview for his team. After eight months of trying relentlessly, I finally made the internal transfer happen.

> **PRO TIP:** Thankfully, you don't need everyone to take a bet on you. Just one will do. Finding that person/ hiring manager/recruiter will take time. Expect multiple rejections before you do. If your resolve and preparation are strong enough, you *will* get someone to take that chance.

## Be realistic

Some transitions are unlikely in the short term. Don't set yourself up for failure by setting unrealistic goals in unrealistic time frames. We overestimate what we can do in one year and underestimate what we can do in 10. You can change your industry, your function, and your geographical location but all three are unlikely to change immediately. Gradual change is often much more sustainable.

Please don't take my suggestion of being realistic to be at odds with dreaming big. Both can coexist with the proper time frame. Dream big and act small by trying to take micro-steps in the right direction.

My first micro-step was setting up a minimum viable product for Network Capital in the form of a Facebook group and observing two things: customer behavior and my own interest level in figuring out the messy challenge of career exploration for millennials. Without this micro-step, Network Capital would have remained an idea in my head.

> **PRO TIP:** Micro-actions compound over time to deliver exponential results. Take the first step and be consistent about it. Urgency in actions, and patience with results, will serve you well.

## Have a backup plan

Create an alternative you can live with when things aren't going as envisioned or planned. It might be somewhere in between your ultimate aspiration and your current state. This can bridge the skill and network gap you might be facing during career transitions. More important, it will set you up on the journey you wish to embark upon.

Today, my backup plan isn't going back to corporate. I have, however, thought through various scenarios for Network Capital. Perhaps it will become a hyper-scalable big tech company, perhaps it will evolve into a more niche offering. I am comfortable with both outcomes as I now realize I am more in love with the problem of career navigation than the solution. Hopefully, I will help solve it. If not, I can help others figure it out.

> **PRO TIP:** Set a time frame. Suppose you want to transition from law to social impact consulting and

making that switch is proving to be difficult, perhaps because of lack of relevant experience. Here
your backup plan could be time-bound. You could
give yourself one year to make the switch from law
to social impact consulting by acquiring the right set
of skills, building a tribe of mentors, and networking
with industry professionals. If it still doesn't work out,
you can rethink your goal or look at accomplishing
it in the longer term if it still interests you.

. . .

Career transitions are complex, and there is usually a lot more
to them than we see on the surface. For me, transitioning from
the corporate lifestyle to that of a scrappy entrepreneur has been
both challenging and rewarding.

I still remember my last day at Microsoft, the day I went back
to the office to submit my badge, laptop, and corporate expense
card. I was giving up a big part of my identity. As I took a walk
across the empty floor bidding adieu to all the wonderful memories and learning experiences, I knew my time here had prepared
me well for the journey ahead.

If you aren't thinking about a career transition today, some
day you will. And when that day comes, my hope is that you
approach it with curiosity, conviction, and commitment. Career
transitions are messy, but they can also turn out to be catalysts
in shaping a future self you will be proud of. There is no way of
guaranteeing success, but not trying might just leave you with
regrets.

## QUICK RECAP

Making a career transition is complicated. The decision to do so requires careful planning and thinking through the why, the what, and the when:

- **Why do you want to change?** Is it the culture of the organization, the people you work with, or is something else bogging you down?

- **What do you want to do?** Conduct a self-assessment. Write down the steps you will need to take that will get you closer to your goals and the problems that you might encounter in doing so.

- **When will the change happen?** Be realistic about the time it can take to make a career transition. Don't set yourself up for failure by setting unrealistic goals.

Adapted from content posted on hbr.org, July 19, 2021.

# Thinking of Quitting Your Job?

by Priscilla Claman

Odds are, at some point in your career, you'll feel like quitting your job. Maybe it will be because of a negative experience—a toxic boss, unfair pay, burnout. But maybe you'll just be eager for a new challenge or ready to move forward in your career.

Regardless of why you may want to leave your organization, don't just quit. It's important to think through how you'll make the move before you make it. Where will you go next? Should you let your boss know what you're planning? How candid can you be about your search?

If you feel ready to quit, ask yourself the following questions to determine the best approach:

# What Are You Looking for in Your Next Position?

This is the first or second question any recruiter will ask you during a job search. If you ask your friends to help with your search, they will likely ask you the same question, too. You may not be 100% sure about your answer, and you may not be aiming to land a particular job title, but take a half hour to come up with some specifics.

Fold a piece of paper into thirds, and then write at the top of each third:

- Things I want to know how to do

- Things I enjoy doing

- Things I never want to do again

Don't agonize over your choices; just fill in whatever comes to mind, like "helping clients solve problems" or "preparing reports" or "mentoring new employees."

You likely won't have a complete picture of what you want, but you will have enough to start your search process. Don't worry if your list changes as you search; just update it from time to time.

> **PRO TIP:** Write down some skills required for a higher-level job in the "Things I want to know how to do" column. This will help you look for a job at a higher level than your current one, advance your career, and get higher pay.

## Can I Find the Job I Want in My Current Organization?

For people who just can't stand the organization they work for, it may make sense to skip this question; but if you think your boss might help you, try to meet with them and ask for new responsibilities or new advancement opportunities. If you can get what you want where you are now, you will get results much more quickly and easily than going through an entire search.

Ask your boss, "Can we meet to talk about my career direction?" Don't just wing it for this meeting. Take some time to think through what you want to say. For example, if you want more responsibility where you are, you might say, "During the pandemic, I had the chance to help with the hiring and onboarding of our new hires. I feel I could make a greater contribution to the department if I had management training and had a chance to be an assistant to you."

Or, if you are interested in making a change outside your department, you might ask for classes or job shadowing opportunities in the area you are targeting—or even an introduction to a manager working in that area of your organization. During the discussion, bring up the potential job transition. If you're interested in accounting, for instance, you could say, "As you know, I've been taking accounting courses for a while now. If I were to target moving to more of an accounting position in a year or so, who do you think I should be talking to? Is that something you would support?"

If you are looking to make a bigger career transition—say, from marketing to finance or from operations to accounting, it's always easier to do so at your current employer, where people know your work, you have direct access to hiring managers in other departments, and you can more easily make the case for your transition.

In the meeting with your manager, don't say you'll leave or threaten to do so; just ask to talk about your career. If your manager is unresponsive to your interests, that's a clue that you should look elsewhere.

## Should I Tell My Boss I Am Looking for a New Job?

In nine out of 10 cases, the answer to this question is: Don't do it. You would be taking a huge risk. Your manager might think, "This person isn't loyal to me or the team" or, "This person isn't here for long, so I'll give the best assignments to people I can trust to be here to complete the work."

If your boss doesn't expect you to be around long, there is a likelihood you will be treated like a temp employee and be given less engaging assignments or excluded from important meetings—all of which may make an already unfulfilling job more difficult to cope with.

By all means, get support from your close nonwork friends while you search, but watch out what you post on social media—it could come back to haunt you. Also, avoid telling any of your colleagues at work. The word is bound to get around your workplace and back to your manager.

## How Can I Get References from My Current Organization If I Am Keeping My Search Confidential?

Usually, you will need three references, including your current manager. But you can ask the organization that is recruiting you not to contact your current manager until they have given you an offer. This is a very common thing to do, but you probably will still need to give them three references up front.

Ask someone who knows your work, like a more senior colleague or team lead, perhaps from a prior job, professional association, or even a client. If you are leaving your first job ever, use references from your most relevant internship or a professor. Or just use the references you used to get your current job. Prepare your references by giving them your résumé. Tell them about the new role and what points you want them to emphasize about you and your work, and give them a heads-up that the recruiter will be in contact via email or phone. And don't forget to thank them and tell them if you got the job.

## What If I Land a New Job and My Current Boss Offers Me a Great Counteroffer?

Think it through carefully before agreeing to stay. It's usually a bad idea. Your boss now knows you've been looking for a new job. This means, moving forward, they may distrust your commitment to the organization. They might fear you will eventually change your mind and leave again, putting you in the situation where your manager treats you like a temp.

Remember that it's easy for your manager to hire a new person to do your job for less pay and lay you off once the new person is fully trained. The only time when it might make sense to accept a counteroffer is if you are immediately offered a new higher-level job, along with a pay increase or some other benefit you really want (like a new location). That might be a good move if the change is immediate, but if you have to wait six months to get it, the world is changing so fast that this may be a promise your boss won't be able to fulfill. So, in my experience, it's best to just say no.

## How Do I Actually Resign?

Resigning in person is the most professional way to quit. Set up a meeting with your boss to discuss your plans, and be sure to give them at least two weeks' notice. After meeting with your manager, follow up with a formal email that includes your current position, a nice thank you, and the date you will be leaving. You don't need to include where you are going or what you will be doing, but you can if you want to. Here's an example:

> I am resigning from my position as Computer Programmer in the Cambridge, Massachusetts, office in two weeks. My last day of work will be October 15. Many thanks for all the guidance and encouragement you and the team have given me at Amazing Corporation. We should arrange a time to go over what you want me to do in the time I have left with Amazing.

There are times when you aren't going to be able to resign in person, like when you work remotely or your manager is away or in another location. In that case, a call or a virtual meeting will be fine. Either way, you will need to talk to your manager about what you should prioritize in your last two weeks and how to let your colleagues and customers know you are leaving. It's the professional thing to do, and it will preserve your reference the next time you change jobs.

## QUICK RECAP

Are you ready to quit your job? Keep these things in mind:

- Before leaving, brainstorm a list of things you want to know how to do, things you enjoy doing, and things you never want to do again. If you can find a job you want at your current company, consider staying.

- Avoid telling your boss that you're thinking of leaving. If your boss doesn't expect you to be around long, you could be passed over for new opportunities.

- If you receive an offer and your boss counteroffers, accept it only if you are immediately offered a new higher-level job with a pay increase.

- When you've decided to officially resign, set up a meeting with your boss to discuss your plans and give at least two weeks' notice.

Adapted from content posted on hbr.org, July 16, 2021.

Want to quit your job with no regrets?
Watch this video:

# Should You Go to Graduate School?

by Tomas Chamorro-Premuzic

So, you're thinking about going back to school. But you're wondering: Will it really be worth your time, energy, and money?

The job market continues to be fiercely competitive. And while employers are starting to highlight the importance of critical soft skills—such as emotional intelligence, resilience, and learnability—as determinants of performance, some of the most in-demand jobs and fastest-growing industries still require graduate credentials.[1]

At the same time, the number of people enrolling in college continues to rise, effectively devaluating the undergraduate degree. In America, one-third of adults are college graduates, a figure that was just 4.6% in the 1940s.[2]

In light of these figures, it is easy to understand why more and more of the workforce is considering going to graduate school. In the United States, the number of graduate students has tripled since the 1970s, and according to some estimates, 27%

of employers now require master's degrees for roles in which his-torically undergraduate degrees sufficed.[3]

What, then, are the motives you should be considering if you are trying to decide whether or not to enroll? How can you deter-mine if the time—and especially the money—required to pur-sue a graduate education will actually pay off or not? Here are some factors to consider:

# Reasons You *Should* Go to Grad School

- *To bump up your salary potential.* It's no secret that people who have graduate school degrees are generally paid more money than those who don't. While a 25% increase in earnings is the average boost people see, attending the top MBA programs can increase your salary by as much as 60% to 150% (whereas a masters in human services or museum sciences will increase your earnings by a mere 10% to 15%).[4]

- *To set a career change in motion.* AI and automation are replacing many roles with others and a growing proportion of workers are being pushed to reskill and upskill to remain relevant. There's no doubt that most of us will have to reinvent ourselves at some point if we want to do the same. If you find yourself in this situation currently, grad school may not be a bad choice. The bigger challenge, however, will be picking what to major in. If you set yourself up to be a strong candidate for jobs that are in high demand, you risk being too late to the game by the time you graduate. For instance, if everyone studies data science in order to fill unfilled vacancies, in a few years there will be a surplus of candidates. A better strategy is to do your research and try to predict what the in-demand roles will be in the future. Further, many graduate programs are starting to teach soft skills, which will prepare you for an uncertain labor market rather than for specific jobs.

- *To follow your passion.* It's not uncommon for people to get stuck in the wrong job as a result of poor career guidance or a lack of self-awareness at a young age—failing to know their interests and potential when they began their careers. This leads to low levels of engagement, performance, and productivity, and high levels of burnout, stress, and alienation. Pursuing your passion, therefore, is not a bad criterion for deciding to go to grad school. After all, people perform better and learn more when their studies align with their values.[5] If you can nurture your curiosity and interests by pursuing rigorous learning, your expertise will be more likely to set you apart from other candidates and increase your chances of ending up in a job you love.

## Reasons You Should *Not* Go to Grad School

- *You can learn for free (or for much less money).* There is a plethora of content—books, videos, podcasts, and more—that are now widely available, at no cost, to the general

public. Arguably, much of this free content mirrors (or
actually is) the material students are studying in grad
school programs. Therefore, if you want a master's degree
simply to gain more knowledge, it's important to recognize
that it is possible to re-create learning experiences
without paying thousands of dollars for a class. Consider
all the things you can learn just by watching YouTube,
assuming you have the discipline and self-control to
focus: coding, digital drawing, UX design, video editing,
and more. Other platforms, such as Udemy and Coursera
can be used to upskill at a more affordable cost than
attending a degree program. Essentially, if your goal is
to acquire a new skill, and that skill can be taught, it
is hard to compete with platforms where experts can
crowdsource, teach, and share content.

- *You may be wasting your time.*  Historically, people have
  learned mostly by doing—and there is a big difference
  between communicating the theoretical experience of
  something and actually going through that experience.
  This is a truth that can't be changed by a graduate (or
  undergraduate) education. In fact, most *Fortune* 500
  firms end up investing substantially to reskill and upskill
  new hires, regardless of their credentials.[6] For instance,
  employers like Google, Amazon, and Microsoft all pointed
  out that learnability—having a hungry mind and being a
  fast and passionate learner—is more important than
  having acquired certain expertise in college.[7] Along the
  same lines, many employers complain that even the best-
  performing graduates will need to learn the most relevant
  job skills, such as leadership and self-management, after

they start their jobs. Oddly, this does not stop employers from paying a premium for college qualifications, including graduate credentials.

- *You will probably go into debt.* For some grad school programs, the ROI is clear, but there's a great deal of variability. It can be challenging to find a program that is certain to boost your income in the short run, particularly if you also want to study something you love. For example, an MBA is more likely to increase your earning potential than a master's in climate change. But if your true passion is climate change, you may end up excelling and having a more lucrative long-term career while you struggle financially in the short term. All of this is to say that if you're not committed to the subject you're studying enough to go into debt for a few years, the risk probably isn't worth the degree.

What is discouraging is that this dilemma would not be a problem at all if:

- Employers started to pay more attention to factors other than a candidate's college degree or formal credentials

- Universities devoted more time to teaching soft skills (and got better at it)

- Universities focused on nurturing a sense of curiosity, which would be a long-term indicator of people's career potential, even for jobs they have never done before

The problem is that employers tend to prioritize the qualifications of a graduate degree (the diploma itself) rather than the experience and education one receives while pursuing it.[8] But assuming the recent trend to buy more and more formal education continues, eventually we can assume that graduate credentials won't be enough for candidates to gain a true competitive advantage. Just like the value of a master's degree is equivalent to the value of an undergraduate degree 30 years ago, if in 30 years a large proportion of the workforce obtains a master's, or PhD, employers may finally be forced to look at talent and potential beyond formal qualifications.

It seems, then, that the decision to go or not to go to grad school is as complex as uncertain, for there are no clear-cut arguments in favor of it or against it. To be sure, it is not easy to predict what the ROI of grad school will be, though the factors outlined here may help you assess your own individual circumstances. Like any big decision in life, this one requires a fair amount of courage and risk taking. In the words of Daniel Kahneman, the Nobel Prize–winning psychologist who pioneered the modern study of decision-making under uncertainty, "Courage is willingness to take the risk once you know the odds. Optimistic over-confidence means you are taking the risk because you don't know the odds. It's a big difference."[9]

## QUICK RECAP

If you're thinking of getting a master's degree, it's important to first consider the reasons you should or shouldn't go to graduate school.

- **Why you should go:** People who have graduate degrees are generally paid more than those who don't, and getting a degree can also help you more easily make a career transition or follow your passion.

- **Why you shouldn't go:** You will likely go into debt from pursuing a master's degree, and some of the information you could learn in school can also be learned online at a lower cost.

---

Adapted from content posted on hbr.org,
January 7, 2020 (#H05CK0).

# What If I Don't Want a Traditional Career Path?

# Four Pieces of Career Advice It's OK to Ignore

by Tomas Chamorro-Premuzic

When you are in the earliest stages of your career, there is no shortage of advice to help you navigate things like how to get hired, make a good impression, and fulfill your wildest job aspirations. But what is talked about less often is the advice that you actually shouldn't follow, which turns out to be a lot of it.

Some of the most common career tips—just be yourself, focus on your strengths, follow your passion—don't pan out in the real world. Even when the advice feels intuitively right, much of the actual data and research suggests that we are probably better off doing the exact opposite.

Here are a few gold standard tips you should probably just ignore, and what you should do instead:

# "Just Be Yourself"

This may be one of the most overused and harmful pieces of career advice ever given. In work settings, especially job interviews, people don't want to see your unfiltered and uninhibited personality. They are more interested in seeing the best version of you—that is, you on your best behavior, telling them what they want to hear, even if it isn't exactly what you want to say. Adhering to social etiquette, showing restraint and self-control, and playing the game of self-presentation will maximize your chances of landing a job.

## What to do instead

In any high-stakes situation, including job interviews, you will be rewarded if you manage and control your public image. Sociologist Erving Goffman's theory on self-presentation highlights this concept—we often act how we want others to see us, even if it is not 100% genuine.[1] The science of social impressions says that this is indeed the best approach. You should read the room and work out what others expect of you.[2] Then tweak your behavior to avoid disappointing them. Be sensitive to context. For instance, if you are speaking to a recruiter at a disruptive tech startup, you should not wear the same outfit you might wear to an interview at a big bank or conservative corporation.

This doesn't mean you need to violate your own principles or be an imposter. It just means you need to be emotionally intelligent enough to respect the social etiquette of the company looking to hire you. Things might be different five years later when you are an established player in the company and have a strong reputation, but you need to play the game before you can break the rules. Your rules may be better, but a job interview is no time to persuade other people of that.

# "Let Your Achievements Speak for Themselves"

The world would be better off if people succeeded because of their competence rather than confidence. In a perfect world, you would not need to spend time self-promoting, self-branding, politicking, and managing up. But sadly, this is not the reality. All style and no substance will get you further than no style and all substance. In the workforce, research has shown time and again that connections, impressions, and showmanship tend to trump talent and potential.[3]

## What to do instead

Your brand is a bigger driver of your career success than your actual work. This means that even the most talented people benefit a lot from managing up—cultivating strong relationships with their bosses, and making sure powerful people see their value. For you, my advice is to learn how to (humbly) be your loudest cheerleader. The ideal scenario is for your boss to think that you are just as modest as you are talented. Being too explicit or assertive can backfire.

Observe people in positions of power and make an effort to understand what problems they're trying to solve. Then show and tell them how you can help. This is a better formula for success than ignoring others and focusing only on your own work. Even the greatest artists in the world, such as van Gogh and Mozart, died poor because they were not focused enough on playing the game of business politics.

## "Focus on Your Strengths"

People generally love this piece of career advice, because it's much easier to follow than the alternative: "Recognize and mitigate your weaknesses." The problem is that strengths are born out of tendencies that come naturally to us—spontaneous parts of ourselves that elevate our status and reputation with others. And while everyone has them, it is virtually impossible to succeed in any area of life unless you learn to keep your weaknesses in check, too.

For example, you can be the smartest person in the world, but if you lack empathy and humility, your intelligence will make you seem arrogant and cold. You could be the most talented writer, but if you have no self-control, you will never produce much work or deliver it on time. Moreover, if overused, your strengths will eventually turn into weaknesses: Too much confidence turns into delusion, a surplus of kindness into conflict avoidance, and extreme ambition into greed.

### What to do instead

Aristotle noted that every virtue is a mean between two extremes. It is better to be somewhat emotional than cold or explosive; it is better to be somewhat curious than closed-minded or reckless;

and it is better to be a little bit creative than unimaginative or eccentric. If your goal is to adapt to the real world and make a strong impression on others—which comes in handy at the start of your career—take this advice instead: Celebrate your strengths, but also do the work of identifying your weaknesses.

All extraordinary achievers are rather self-critical. To a large degree, their very ambition is the result of constantly attempting to overcome their limitations, and their inability to be satisfied just with their achievements. Similarly, when you know what your weaknesses are, you will experience a healthy degree of discomfort. That discomfort may drive you to get better—to close the gap between the person you are and the person you want to be. You'll get farther, faster.

## "Follow Your Passion"

While it helps to have a clear idea of what you want to do in life, following your passion is often only a winning formula if your passion aligns with job market demand and your actual talent. It is also true that passions are more ephemeral than we tend to think: This year you may be passionate about photography, but next year you might be passionate about science, writing, or animation. In most cases, if you only look for opportunities in industries that you love, instead of broadening your perspective and considering those that will make you grow, you end up sacrificing jobs that could advance your career down the line.

You also give up an important chance at self-discovery—that is, a chance to learn more about what you want and don't want and to stumble upon new things you may be good at or enjoy. Remember that following your passion can be a protective strategy, one that allows you to stay within your comfort zone and play to your strengths, while it hampers your development.

## What to do instead

Usually, the younger you are, the more trade-offs you have to make. In your twenties, you should think hard about matching your interests and potential to available opportunities and seize the ones that will help you learn and grow. In your thirties, you might want to shift your focus from earning short-term rewards to making a longer-term impact. At both stages, it is wise to be flexible. Treat your strong interests as nice-to-haves, but put them on standby until the chance arrives to unleash them in a productive way. In the end, it is less useful to follow your passion than it is to find people who are passionately devoted to helping you grow. The good news is that the trade-offs decrease with age.

In short, the best thing you can do right now is make the best possible choices. This means being open, and trying to carefully assess the pros and cons each path that opens to you might present. What you value is key, and you should never violate your own moral compass. After that, your success chances will probably increase if you maximize fit between your potential, interests, and opportunities.

### QUICK RECAP

Some of the most common career tips don't pan out in the real world. Here are four you should ignore—and what to do instead.

- Don't: Just be yourself. Do: Be the best version of yourself.

- Don't: Let your achievements speak for themselves. Do: Build a personal brand.

- Don't: Focus only on your strengths. Do: Mitigate your weaknesses, too.

- Don't: Follow your passion. Do: Explore areas outside your main interests.

---

Adapted from content posted on hbr.org, October 15, 2020.

# You Don't Have to Become the Boss to Grow in Your Career

by Anne Sugar

Most of us grew up thinking that in order to be truly successful, we had to be the boss. But this is a myth. You don't need to be a manager to have a lucrative and fulfilling career.

The professional landscape has changed dramatically in the last several decades. With advances in technology, there are countless opportunities for people who want to focus their growth on developing specific skill sets and technical expertise. Many of these paths don't involve managing a team.

Here are some methods to grow your career if being the boss is just not for you.

## Understand Your Limitations

First, know that if you choose not to go into management, you have to be realistic about your path moving forward. There are certain opportunities that won't be available to you. But when one door closes, another opens. It's useful to understand and weigh your options based on the following parameters:

You probably won't be promoted into high-power positions in the C-suite or as the head of a department. People who grow into these roles usually do so through years of experience managing people, and they are often responsible for running teams of their own.

You probably will have the opportunity to grow as an individual contributor, develop expertise in your field, and become the best at what you do. Because you are not formally in charge of others, you'll have more time to focus on your personal contributions to an organization or industry and master a particular skill set.

Keep in mind that some industries are better designed to develop individual contributors, while others have few growth opportunities for people uninterested in management. For instance: In telecommunications, consulting, publishing, and technology, leaders can climb the ranks and even land senior roles without directly leading a team. By contrast, sectors like advertising or product management more readily promote those who are interested in people leadership.

## Define What Success Means to You

What does success look like for you? There isn't a right or wrong answer when it comes to what makes you happy. In fact, career success can take on many different forms: having a good work-life balance, exercising your creativity, or making a lot of money—to name just a few. Your version of success depends on your goals.

If you're not sure what your goals are yet, block out some reflection time on your calendar. Write down specific instances when you've been happy at work or in school. Think about moments when you were completely enveloped, when time flew by because you were focused or content, energized or inspired. Now do the opposite. Write down moments when your work was boring or draining.

Look at what you've written. Do you notice any patterns?

After contemplating, you will start to see a trend. For example, maybe you'll notice that focusing on creative work like content ideation drives your motivation. Or maybe you'll find that you prefer heads-down, technical work that requires concentration and a solo working environment. Whatever you discover, start to think about how you can do that more often in your career.

## Be Proactive

After you've defined what makes you feel happy and successful as a sole contributor, look for opportunities where you can step into this kind of role. To do this, you will need to be proactive.

You may need to create an opportunity for yourself that your manager can help refine. A good first step is developing a proposal that outlines the opportunity you would like to initiate and move ahead with over time.

To start, ask yourself the following questions:

- What value do I add to the company?

- How do I help the company reach its goals?

- Can I cite any metrics to demonstrate the value of my impact?

- What would my role look like if I continued as a sole contributor?

- As the company grows, how do I see myself growing within it?

Use your answers to these questions to draft your proposal. Think of this as a plan for your future growth that you can present to your manager during a performance review or one-on-one discussion. Finding the right time to talk to your manager is crucial; you want their full attention. For example, don't schedule a lunch meeting at the end of the quarter, when your manager has many other demands to sort through.

One leader I spoke with decided that, after a bumpy road as a manager, she wanted to be a subject matter expert in her department. In this new role, she hoped to focus on guiding and developing strategy. But in order to switch positions, she first needed to prove to her manager that the work she hoped to do as an individual contributor would be of value to her team.

She wrote up a short proposal stating her current skill set and what she would be responsible for in this new role. To connect the dots for her manager, she explained how those responsibilities would help support the larger goals of the company, including three specific and attainable tasks for which she could be responsible.

Over the course of many conversations, she and her manager refined her initial proposal for the role. They came up with a few goals that would be mutually beneficial to both her department and her career development as an individual contributor. Had this leader failed to take the initiative and present a clear picture of the work she wanted to do and why, she would never have landed the role she really wanted.

# Keep Learning

There are plenty of successful people (and even leaders) who have chosen not to be managers—most of whom are within your reach. Dig through your LinkedIn network to find professionals who are doing what you would like to do. Learn from them— read their posts, track their journeys, and personally reach out. They may be willing to chat with you about how they ended up in their current roles.

When you message them, be personal and direct. Try to mention one thing you admire about their work or career path and ask one specific question to initiate the conversation. (Keep it short—you don't want to create more work for this person.) If they respond, you can start to build out the relationship over time.

For example, your message may look like this:

Hi [name]—

I really enjoyed your recent post about [topic]. My name is [name] and I'm currently a [job title] at [company], but I have a strong interest in [industry or role], which I know is your area of expertise. I'd love to learn more about your career journey and how you ended up where you are. [Include a specific question about their journey here]?

## Periodically, Check In with Yourself

Each year, plan on taking an hour to think about your current role and where you see your career going. Keep it simple and ask yourself the following questions:

- How did I track toward my goals this year?

- What does my manager say about how I'm doing?

- What has been going right?

- What can I work on?

- What is the gap in my skill set?

- Does my career still align with my values?

With these buckets, you can better determine how to move forward—no matter what path you choose. Your definition of success may change over time, and you can always switch directions and decide you want to take a different path. Spend the quiet time to learn, look for patterns, and understand your strengths. There are many avenues to growing your career. With planning and deliberate action, you can set yourself on a path that makes you feel confident, energized, and excited.

## QUICK RECAP

How do you grow in your career if you don't want to become a manager?

- Be realistic about your path moving forward. You probably won't be promoted into high-power positions, but you will have the opportunity to develop deep expertise in your field.

- Define what success looks like for you: having a good work-life balance, exercising your creativity, or making a lot of money, for example.

- Look for opportunities that will help you reach that vision and develop a proposal for your manager on how you plan to pursue those opportunities.

- Each year, check in with yourself about your current role and where you see your career going.

Adapted from content posted on hbr.org,
September 8, 2021.

What is it like to take on a management role
for the first time? Listen to this podcast:

# Should You Really Be Indispensable at Work?

by Liz Wiseman

You may have heard the advice to make yourself indispensable at work. Sure, it sounds smart. Beyond the obvious plus of having a secure source of income, knowing that you're needed may provide you with a sense of safety and ease your mental load (especially when layoffs are on the table).

But unfortunately—and despite the cacophony of articles swearing by this approach—it's often unrealistic and shortsighted.

For the last several years, I've researched how top workplace contributors think and behave.[1] Through interviews and surveys with employees around the world, I've found, for most people, the desire to have our work matter and make an impact is universal. I've also found that when that desire translates into a drive to make ourselves indispensable, we put our long-term career growth at risk.

## When Being Indispensable Backfires

Consider the experience of Paige (not her real name), an HR manager at a high-growth tech startup. Paige had her hands in everything. She helped build out the HR department and ensure her team could keep pace with rapid hiring. When her colleagues in finance and payroll were overloaded, she took on the extra work. She was scrappy and learned to do things herself. Even as she onboarded capable specialists, she kept the most critical tasks on her to-do list. She produced offer letters and handled employment verifications. Stakeholders depended on her. Her employees counted on her to approve their vacations and cover their work. She was a favorite of the boss (the CFO).

But as the company grew, and HR responsibilities expanded, Paige couldn't let go of the reins. Her newly hired staff grew tired of handling only menial tasks, and many of them left for better opportunities. Paige was vital—indispensable even—but she was also a bottleneck. Employees couldn't close on house purchases when she fell behind processing employment verifications. The CEO couldn't extend an offer letter to a critical hire because Paige was on a rare vacation. Stress and exhaustion became a way of life until she suffered a collapse of mental and physical health. Months later, she returned to a smaller job that continued to shrink in scope and impact.

Paige's experience is a reminder that the quest to be absolutely necessary is often limiting, both for the individual and the organization. Why?

- Making yourself irreplaceable can tether you to your job and compromise your well-being. Additionally, it reduces potential for growth. If no one else can handle your job, you won't be able to step up into new opportunities as they arise—you are too critical where you are. If there's no one strong enough on the bench to replace you, it's hard to move on to a bigger arena.

- There are important implications for your success as a leader. When you position yourself as a gatekeeper or go-to person, it's easy to become a know-it-all and limit your effectiveness. You can deem yourself so vital that you become diminishing—someone who is smart and capable, but who shuts down the intelligence and capabilities of the people whom you lead. When staff are chronically underutilized, apathy sets in and people lower their ambitions, doing only the minimum. You, as an indispensable leader, will become costly to your organization and ultimately sabotage your own career.

So, how do you create value and secure your position without overstepping? While being indispensable is often a problem, being easily replaceable isn't ideal either. What's the right balance?

## How to Be Valuable at Work

The most valuable contributors pay attention to what's important and do the job that needs to be done—right now. They aren't just experts and know-it-alls. They are learn-it-alls who adapt and change as the needs of the organization change. They eliminate bottlenecks and reduce friction points that slow down progress. Perhaps most importantly, their value doesn't just come from the work they do themselves. They are integral to teams—a part of a larger whole—and their presence helps to maximize and multiply the talent of the entire group.

In other words, your value at work will grow if you replicate yourself rather than protect your scarce skills. By developing others around you, you increase the impact and progress of the work that needs to be done, protect your mental health, find a stable work-life balance, and most important, you become an invaluable asset to your team and the company at large.

To become this employee, start by practicing three things:

1. *Figure out what needs to be done and do it without being asked.* While we often think of bosses as power-hungry dictators, the truth is that most managers dislike having to tell people what to do. In our survey of 170 managers about what employee behaviors they most appreciate, the number one response was: "When people do things without being asked."[2] People who take the lead and show initiative get deputized by their leaders, which means they gain valuable leadership experience and influence, and can advance to larger roles.

   How do you figure out what needs to be done? Listen for ambient problems—low-grade, persistent problems where the organization can make marked improvement with a little bit of leadership and focus. What is everyone complaining about but not doing anything about? Or notice the things that frustrate your manager or customers and surprise them with a fix.

2. *Fill a leadership vacuum.* Look for situations that lack clear leadership and step up to fill the void. Here's an example

of two all-too-common situations that could use some direction:

- *Unclear meetings.* It is estimated that 63% of meetings have no planned agenda.[3] When you see this happening, take charge. Provide the much-needed clarity by suggesting the group agree on intended outcomes for the meeting. Before the meeting, send out an agenda to help people prepare. At the start, set the tone by saying something like, "What is the most important thing for us to accomplish during this meeting?" This will give people an idea of what you need to accomplish within that time frame and set you apart as the person who actually gets things done.

- *Unsung heroes.* Most employees express a need to be recognized, by their boss, peers, and clients; however, according to a Glassdoor survey, only two-thirds of employees said that their bosses showed them enough appreciation.[4] You can fill this leadership void by speaking up to recognize the contributions of your peers or collaborators, especially those who work behind the scenes. Elevating the contributions of others gets them the credit they deserve, but it helps you too—research shows that amplifying others' voices boosts your own status and engenders the trust you need to lead without authority.[5] Try saying, "I just wanted to take a moment to thank Hala for her social media expertise last week. It's helped us gain 10K new followers!"

3. *Contribute where you have unique strengths.* The most valuable contributors don't chase after any and every need

or shiny object; rather they look for a match between a critical need and their own deepest capabilities—a concept I call native genius. When people use their greatest strengths in service to something larger than themselves, there's usually an extra spark of brilliance where everyone benefits. Know what you do best and offer that capability to your colleagues freely. You might even create a "User's Guide to You" to help your leaders and colleagues know how to use you at your best, creating the greatest value add for the organization and for you.

. . .

Certainly, all people have value and bring capability to their jobs; however, some make themselves more valuable than others. It's rarely because you can't function without them; it's because you would never want to lose them. They not only play big; they help other people play bigger too. So, instead of making yourself irreplaceable, make your most valuable contribution.

## QUICK RECAP

The quest to be absolutely necessary at work can be limiting, both for you and for your organization. Instead of making yourself irreplaceable, try to make yourself valuable.

- **Figure out what needs to be done and do it without being asked.** What is everyone complaining about but not doing anything about? Try to fix it.

- **Fill a leadership vacuum.** Look for situations that lack clear leadership and step up to fill the void. For example, set agendas for meetings currently with no direction.

- **Contribute where you have unique strengths.** The most valuable contributors don't chase after every shiny object— they look for a match between a critical need and their capabilities.

Adapted from content posted on hbr.org, September 20, 2022.

# The Case for Making Terrible Career Choices

by Ruchika Tulshyan

Ask me about my biggest career foible and I'll usually respond with the clichéd "There are no regrets, only lessons."

But that's not entirely true. There will always be one career decision I made—one that altered the course of my life quite significantly—that I often come back to. Part "that was a terrible decision" and part "wow, I can't believe I survived that."

It was moving to Mumbai from New York in my early twenties.

If I back up a little, I'm not quite sure what sparked my decision to apply for an internship at a business news organization halfway across the world. I was a recent journalism school graduate in New York, interning at a well-known magazine, surrounded by supportive bosses and the possibility of a full-time job offer. I had no business applying for a role at a company that valued balance sheets and market knowledge over writing chops. Worse, I'd have to start from scratch in Mumbai, a city

I barely knew outside the yearly trips I made to visit my maternal grandparents.

Needless to say, I landed the internship, and it rolled in with more money in Indian rupees than I was making in NYC. Two suitcases in hand, I made the move to Mumbai, where I planned to live as a paying guest in an elderly woman's house for the duration of the fall.

Everything about the move was a disaster. I struggled to settle into a new culture, both the country's and the organization's. My hours as a journalist covering the opening of the financial markets meant I had to be in at 6 a.m. My boss barely looked in my direction, let alone mentored me. I worked with one man who stood too close, close enough that I could feel his breath on my neck when he looked over my shoulder at my screen, but discreetly enough that I couldn't call HR.

I struggled in every way—never measuring up to any of my absent boss's expectations, never fully enjoying (or at times, even understanding) the work I did. But now, I can look back more than a decade later, and say I'm happy I took the risk.

Sometimes terrible career decisions are worth making, and we all, at some point, are going to make them. When you take on a job or project that you quickly realize is a mistake, it's easy to lose hope. It can eat away at your confidence and sense of purpose. But if you focus on the long view, I'd argue that working through what you *don't* want can bring you that much closer to what you do. Ultimately, it can even set you up to design a career that fulfills you.

I've thought many times about this experience and the lessons I learned from the internship, many of which were key to building the career I have today. If you're in a job or an internship that feels like a drag, working with a manager who doesn't have your back or learning the ropes in an unfamiliar place, there are ways to navigate all this and more to your advantage (and maintain your sanity).

## Build Relationships with Your Coworkers

Often when we start new jobs, we're expected to be tough. But building relationships—even professional ones—takes vulnerability. We often forget this when we already have a support system close by.

With no family, friends, or network to rely on in Mumbai, I had to be vulnerable in ways I hadn't been before. I threw myself headfirst into meeting colleagues, forming connections, and saying yes to new experiences—new food, new music, and even a new caffeine habit. (In place of coffee, I consumed endless cups of chai brought around by the office chaiwallah.)

While the in-office support I received was invaluable, I also benefited in countless other ways. The easy, laid-back attitude of certain colleagues taught me how to manage my nerves on breaking news deadlines. Despite my absent boss, the sponsorship of senior journalists ensured I was learning the ropes and getting access to stretch projects.

Though I didn't anticipate it then, I continue to keep in touch with many of the people who supported me through that time. Thanks to social media, I'll always have a network of international journalists to call upon.

**The takeaway:** The time I spent overseas reminds me, even now, of the importance of investing in professional relationships.

I couldn't have survived my time there without the good humor and kindness of my peers. It's essential to invest in relationships with your coworkers—they are the ones who may make an otherwise difficult experience worthwhile.

## Ask for Help

Speaking of kindness, I learned to ask for help from my support system often. When my manager ignored me, it was my peers with whom I celebrated my small victories, like filing my first breaking news story. When a shady realtor tried to extort me for money (true story), my colleagues gave me the emotional reinforcements I needed not to be bullied further.

In retrospect, I wish I had asked for more help. Maybe I should have sat down with my always-harried boss, shared my needs, and asked him if there was any way I could get extra support, from learning how to succeed at the organization to more tactical advice around how to file stronger stories.

**The takeaway:** Pride got in the way back then, and I was miserable for much of the job, but the importance of asking for help when you need it has been ingrained in my mind since. Learn from my experience, and speak up—the worst someone can tell you is no.

## Take Note of Your Nonnegotiables

Being a woman in any corporate environment isn't without its challenges. Being a female employee in a completely new country was truly a ball of contradictions. I had to recalibrate my understandings of work culture and the general attitude toward the role of women in society—including the workplace. On the one hand, I worked with some incredible male colleagues who sponsored and mentored me, shared resources, and treated me with utmost dignity and respect. Then there were the others—the men who leered in the office, who infringed on my personal space, who avoided eye contact with me because of my gender.

In my early twenties, I didn't always know how to stand up for myself, but encountering sexism up close, it became clear that an inclusive, gender-balanced work environment was a nonnegotiable for me. Later in my career, when I experienced a similarly exclusionary work culture in the United States, I quickly and clearly knew I had to walk away from the job, even when others urged me to press on.

**The takeaway:** My experience in India had made it clear that working in an inclusive workplace is a nonnegotiable for me. Pay attention to your own experiences in your early career, especially the more challenging ones. What are your nonnegotiables? The more you understand about what you are and aren't willing to compromise on, the more easily you'll be able to craft the kind of career you want in the future.

## Celebrate Your Resilience

For one of my most memorable assignments, I had to hop on the Mumbai local train with a veteran reporter and speak to vendors in large spice markets about commodity prices. The other journalist didn't speak the local language, so I became the translator. For the first time, I was learning how to report a long-form story while operating in a different language.

All my work experiences in other countries until that point—the United States, the United Kingdom, and Singapore—hadn't prepared me for that kind of challenge. But after a grueling day in the heat of an unfamiliar territory, I realized I was more resilient and adaptable than I thought at that age.

What built that resilience even further is how, when I was left out of the byline, I stood up for myself and asked the editors and the reporter to include me. I had contributed significantly to the final piece and should have been recognized for my work. They ultimately refused (which reinforced that it was time to walk away), but I learned that if I didn't advocate for myself, no one else would.

**The takeaway:** In the moments that feel the hardest, make a list (either mentally or on paper) of the triumphs you've collected through the most difficult times. For me, these would have been as straightforward as "Today, I walked to my office without getting lost." Celebrate all the ways you can work through adversity, in the big and small ways, because they eventually add up to overcoming the most trying challenges.

## Reflect on What You've Learned

Mercifully, no hardship will last forever. When I look back, I found solace in continuing to work through the difficult times and constantly asking myself, "What's the lesson here?" Even when I was lonely in my single room in another woman's flat, I comforted myself knowing that this was a once-in-a-lifetime opportunity, and I had the choice to make a change. Most of all, I learned the importance of working in cultures other than the one I grew up in and learning to be humble, flexible, and adaptable.

I left Mumbai within three months, replete with more *shouldn'ts* than *shoulds*, and with a lifetime of lessons and memories.

**The takeaway:** If I had to go back, I would do it all over again.

. . .

Now, over a decade later, as a working mother settled in a comfortable, (mostly) drama-free career and life, I know I can't take a leap into the unknown in the same way I did back then. But many of you can—and should. You have the power to work outside your comfort zone, whether moving to a new industry, city, or country—especially if you're in a time of your life when taking calculated risks could pay off big time.

Take it from me, the hard times don't last, but the growth, the relationships, and the resilience all do.

## QUICK RECAP

Sometimes, terrible career decisions are worth making. If you're in a job or internship that feels like a mistake, here's how to use the experience to your advantage:

- **Focus on your relationships.** Make an effort to get close with your coworkers and build your network.

- **Ask for help.** Don't let pride get in the way. Speak up if you need support. The worst thing someone can say is no.

- **Take note of your nonnegotiables.** Knowing what you are and aren't willing to compromise on will help you craft the career you want.

- **Celebrate your resilience.** Be proud of your big and small wins—the challenges you've overcome will help you be more resilient in the future.

- **Reflect on what you've learned.** As you hit roadblocks throughout your career, always ask yourself: "What's the lesson here?"

---

Adapted from content posted on hbr.org,
November 1, 2021.

How can you bounce back from career setbacks?
Listen to this podcast:

# NOTES

## Introduction

1. Akane Otani, "Your Lifetime Earnings Are Decided in the First 10 Years of Your Career," *Bloomberg*, February 9, 2015, https://www.bloomberg.com /news/articles/2015-02-09/your-lifetime-earnings-are-decided-in-the-first-10 -years-of-your-career.

## Chapter 4

1. Devin Tomb, "72% of Muse Survey Respondents Say They've Experienced 'Shift Shock,'" The Muse, August 30, 2022, https://www.themuse.com /advice/shift-shock-muse-survey-2022.

## Chapter 5

1. Kenneth A. Couch and Robert Fairlee, "Last Hired, First Fired? Black-White Unemployment and the Business Cycle," *Demography* 47, no. 1 (February 2010): 227–247, https://www.ncbi.nlm.nih.gov/pmc/articles/PMC3000014/.

2. Kathryn E. W. Himmelstein and Hannah Brückner, "Criminal-Justice and School Sanctions Against Nonheterosexual Youth: A National Longitudinal Study," *Pediatrics* 127, no. 1 (January 2011): 49–57, https://www.ncbi.nlm.nih .gov/pmc/articles/PMC3375466/.

3. Adam Bryant, "Google's Quest to Build a Better Boss," *New York Times*, March 12, 2011, https://www.nytimes.com/2011/03/13/business/13hire.html.

4. Shirin Eskandani, "The Key to Creating Your Best Life (Best of WHC)," *Wholehearted Coaching: The Podcast*, https://www.wholehearted-coaching.com /podcast/your-best-life-best-of-whc.

## Chapter 7

1. Hans Georg Wolff and Klaus Moser, "Effects of Networking on Career Success: A Longitudinal Study," *Journal of Applied Psychology* 94, no. 1 (2009): 196–206, http://homepages.se.edu/cvonbergen/files/2013/01/Effects-of -Networking-on-Career-Success_A-Longitudinal-Study.pdf.

2. Larry Kim, "How to Write the Perfect LinkedIn Connection Request," Customers.ai, https://customers.ai/articles/linkedin-invitation-etiquette.

3. Robert B. Cialdini, *Influence: The Psychology of Persuasion*, rev. ed. (New York: HarperCollins Business Essentials, 2006).

## Chapter 9

1. "Learning in Networks," LibreTexts Social Sciences, https://socialsci .libretexts.org/Bookshelves/Education_and_Professional_Development /Teaching_Crowds_-_Learning_and_Social_Media_(Dron_and_Anderson) /05%3A_Learning_in_Networks.

2. Adam Grant, "We Don't Just Need to Connect—We Need to Reconnect," *New York Times*, April 24, 2020, https://www.nytimes.com/2020/04/24 /smarter-living/reconnecting-with-people.html.

3. Dorie Clark, *The Long Game: How to Be a Long-Term Thinker in a Short-Term World* (Boston: Harvard Business Review Press, 2021).

4. "Active Listening," Fast Facts, http://gwep.usc.edu/wp-content/uploads /2020/03/FastFacts-Telephone-Skills-Training-Active-Listening.pdf.

## Chapter 11

1. "The Nine Enneagram Type Descriptions," Enneagram Institute, https://www.enneagraminstitute.com/type-descriptions.

2. "What Is DiSC?," disc profile, https://www.discprofile.com/what-is-disc; "LIFO Surveys," LIFO Life Orientations, https://lifo.co/getting-started-lifo-process /lifo-survey/; "Big Five Personality Test," Open-Source Psychometrics Project, https://openpsychometrics.org/tests/IPIP-BFFM/; "16 Personality Factors Test," https://openpsychometrics.org/tests/16PF.php; "Motives, Values, Preferences Inventory," Hogan Assessments, https://www.hoganassessments.com/assessment /motives-values-preferences-inventory/.

3. The Passion Test, https://www.thepassiontest.com/about-the-passion-test.

## Chapter 12

1. "Jeff Bezos—Regret Minimization Framework," YouTube, https://youtu .be/jwG_qR6XmDQ?si=bz6Aac1EPldT1iJ9.

2. Kevin Kelley, "1,000 True Fans," The Technium, March 4, 2008, https://kk .org/thetechnium/1000-true-fans/.

3. Marie Forleo, *Everything Is Figureoutable* (New York: Penguin, 2020).

## Chapter 14

1. Emily Rolen, "Occupational Employment Projections Through the Perspective of Education and Training," U.S. Bureau of Labor Statistics, https:// www.bls.gov/spotlight/2019/education-projections/pdf/education-projections.pdf.

2. Reid Wilson, "Census: More Americans Have College Degrees Than Ever Before," *The Hill*, April 3, 2017, https://thehill.com/homenews/state-watch/326995-census-more-americans-have-college-degrees-than-ever-before/.

3. Jon Marcus, "Graduate Programs Have Become a Cash Cow for Struggling Colleges. What Does That Mean for Students?," *NewsHour*, PBS, September 18, 2017, https://www.pbs.org/newshour/education/graduate-programs-become-cash-cow-struggling-colleges-mean-students; Lydia Dishman, "How the Master's Degree Became the New Bachelor's in the Hiring World," *Fast Company*, March 17, 2016, https://www.fastcompany.com/3057941/how-the-masters-degree-became-the-new-bachelors-in-the-hiring-world.

4. Cecilia Capuzzi Simon, "R.O.I.," *New York Times*, July 22, 2011, https://www.nytimes.com/2011/07/24/education/edlife/edl-24roi-t.html.

5. D. Scott DeRue and Frederick P. Morgeson, "Stability and Change in Person-Team and Person-Role Fit over Time: The Effects of Growth Satisfaction, Performance, and General Self-Efficacy," *Journal of Applied Psychology* 92, no. 5 (2007): 1242–1253, https://psycnet.apa.org/record/2007-12832-005.

6. Allison Dulin Salisbury, "The Rise of Outskilling: Why Are a Growing Number of Employers Preparing Workers for Their Next Job?," *Forbes*, November 18, 2019, https://www.forbes.com/sites/allisondulinsalisbury/2019/11/18/the-rise-of-outskilling-why-are-a-growing-number-of-employers-preparing-workers-for-their-next-job/.

7. Sophie von Stumm, Benedikt Hell, and Tomas Chamorro-Premuzic, "The Hungry Mind: Intellectual Curiosity Is the Third Pillar of Academic Performance," *Perspectives on Psychological Science* 6, no. 6 (October 14, 2011): 574–588, https://journals.sagepub.com/doi/full/10.1177/1745691611421204.

8. Tomas Chamorro-Premuzic and Becky Frankiewicz, "6 Reasons Why Higher Education Needs to Be Disrupted," hbr.org, November 19, 2019, https://hbr.org/2019/11/6-reasons-why-higher-education-needs-to-be-disrupted.

9. "Nobel Laureate Debunks Economic Theory," *Forbes*, November 6, 2002, https://www.forbes.com/2002/11/06/cx_da_1106nobel1.html.

## Chapter 15

1. Erving Goffman, *The Presentation of Self in Everyday Life* (New York: Doubleday, 1959).

2. Liad Uziel, "Rethinking Social Desirability Scales: From Impression Management to Interpersonally Oriented Self-Control," *Perspectives on Psychological Science* 5, no. 3 (May 2010): 243–262, https://journals.sagepub.com/doi/10.1177/1745691610369465.

3. Tomas Chamorro-Premuzic, *Why Do So Many Incompetent Men Become Leaders?* (Boston: Harvard Business Review Press, 2019).

## Chapter 17

1. "Research Process," Impact Players, The Wiseman Group, https://impactplayersbook.com/wp-content/uploads/2021/10/impact-players-research-process.pdf.
2. "Research Process," Impact Players, The Wiseman Group.
3. Bryan Kitch, "How to Create Effective Meeting Agendas," Mural, June 10, 2022, https://www.mural.co/blog/how-to-create-meeting-agendas.
4. "Employers To Retain Half of Their Employees Longer If Bosses Showed More Appreciation; Glassdoor Survey," Glassdoor, November 13, 2013, https://www.glassdoor.com/employers/blog/employers-to-retain-half-of-their-employees-longer-if-bosses-showed-more-appreciation-glassdoor-survey/.
5. Kristin Bain, Tamar A. Kreps, Nathan L. Meikle, and Elizabeth R. Tenney, "Amplifying Voice in Organizations," *Academy of Management Journal* 64, no. 4 (September 13, 2021): 1288–1312, https://journals.aom.org/doi/abs/10.5465/amj.2018.0621.

# INDEX

# ABOUT THE CONTRIBUTORS

**MIMI ABOUBAKER** is an entrepreneur and writer. Most recently, she founded Perfect Strangers, the largest coronavirus crisis response initiative in the United States, which delivered over 3 million meals in partnership with nonprofits and government agencies. Prior to entrepreneurial endeavors, she spent time in finance at Goldman Sachs and Morgan Stanley. For more tips on leaning in on career and life, follow her on X/Twitter @mimi_aboubaker and visit her website at www.mimiaboubaker.com.

**UTKARSH AMITABH** is the founder and CEO of Network Capital, one of the world's largest mentorship platforms, which empowers more than 7.5 million school students and 200,000 young professionals to build meaningful careers. Before becoming an entrepreneur, Utkarsh shaped critical public-private partnerships at Microsoft for seven years across the United States, Europe, and India. He was part of the team that built India's first smart village, which was recognized in the Prime Minister's *Book of Pioneering Innovations*. Utkarsh studied moral philosophy at the University of Oxford and earned his MBA from INSEAD. He is the author of two bestselling books, *The Seductive Illusion of Hard Work* and *Passion Economy and the Side Hustle Revolution*.

**JAHNA BERRY** is an award-winning journalist and leadership coach who has written about leadership for *Mother Jones* and

*OpenNews*. She was a featured speaker at events for the National Association of Gay and Lesbian Journalists, *Wired*, University of Missouri's School of Journalism, and the News Product Alliance. She is the Chief Operating Officer at *Mother Jones*.

**ROXANNE CALDER** is the author of *Employable: 7 Attributes to Assuring Your Working Future*. She is also the founder and managing director of EST10, one of Sydney's most successful administration recruitment agencies. Roxanne is passionate about uncovering people's potential and watching their careers soar.

**TOMAS CHAMORRO-PREMUZIC** is the Chief Innovation Officer at ManpowerGroup, a professor of business psychology at University College London and at Columbia University, cofounder of deepersignals.com, and an associate at Harvard's Entrepreneurial Finance Lab. He is the author of *Why Do So Many Incompetent Men Become Leaders? (and How to Fix It)*, upon which his TEDx Talk was based. His latest book is *I, Human: AI, Automation, and the Quest to Reclaim What Makes Us Unique*. Find him at www.drtomas.com.

**PRISCILLA CLAMAN** is a retired human resources executive and career consultant. She is a contributor to the *HBR Guide to Getting the Right Job*.

**IRINA COZMA** is a career and executive coach who supports professionals to have better career adventures. She coached hundreds of *Fortune* 500 executives from global organizations like Salesforce, Hitachi, and Abbott. Irina also coaches clients at startups and students in the Physician Executive MBA at the University of Tennessee. Find her at www.irinacozma.com.

**KRISTI DEPAUL** is a Tel Aviv–based entrepreneur and content marketing expert whose writing empowers aspiring professionals to succeed in the ever-changing landscape of work. Her articles have appeared in top international publications, including *HBR's 10 Must Reads 2024: The Definitive Management Ideas of the Year*, and have been cited by leading think tanks and academicians. She serves as CEO of Founders, a globally distributed content agency that supports influential educational and workforce development organizations across the globe. A longtime proponent of remote work, Kristi has repeatedly been named one of 50 international Remote Innovators in the Remote Influencer Report and remains an ardent advocate for enhancing others' social and economic mobility through location-independent employment.

**MICHELLE GIBBINGS** is bringing back the happy to workplace culture. The award-winning author of three books and a global keynote speaker, she's on a mission to help leaders, teams, and organizations create successful workplaces where people thrive and progress is accelerated.

**ANTOINETTE OGLETHORPE** is a consultant, coach, speaker, and author with 30 years' experience developing leaders for multinational organizations. She is a Chartered Fellow of the CIPD, a member of the Association for Coaching, and a member of the Institute of Leadership. Antoinette's latest book is *Confident Career Conversations: Empower Your Employees for Career Growth and Retention*.

**SEAN O'KEEFE** is an award-winning professor, researcher, and sought-after speaker on creating social capital, career readiness, internships, and jobs. He is the author of *Launch Your Career: How ANY Student Can Create Relationships with Professionals and Land the Jobs and Internships They Want*. He is the founder and partner of Career Launch (www.careerlaunch.academy), a social enterprise that partners with colleges and career programs to measure career readiness and equitably scale students' ability to create professional relationships and launch effective job or internship searches in the hidden job market.

**JANET T. PHAN** is the founder of Thriving Elements, a global nonprofit that connects underserved, underrepresented girls with STEM mentors. She is the author of *Boldly You*, a story about discovering what you're capable of when you show up for yourself. She is also a senior technical program manager working to get affordable and reliable broadband to unserved and underserved communities globally. Her TEDx Talk is entitled "3 Key Elements to a Thriving Mentorship."

**DEBORAH GRAYSON RIEGEL** is a professional speaker, executive coach, and workshop facilitator, as well as a communication and presentation skills coach. She teaches leadership communication at Duke University's Fuqua School of Business and has taught for Wharton Business School, Columbia Business School's Women in Leadership Program, and Peking University's International MBA Program. She is the author of *Overcoming Overthinking: 36 Ways to Tame Anxiety for Work, School, and Life* and the bestselling *Go to Help: 31 Strategies to Offer, Ask for, and Accept Help*.

**APRIL RINNE** is a World Economic Forum Young Global Leader and ranked one of the 50 Leading Female Futurists in the world by *Forbes*. She is a change navigator who helps individuals and organizations rethink and reshape their relationships with change, uncertainty, and a world in flux. She's a trusted adviser, speaker, investor, adventurer (100-plus countries), insatiable handstander, and author of *Flux: 8 Superpowers for Thriving in Constant Change*.

**SUSAN STELTER** is the cofounder and the former Chief People Officer at West Monroe, a digital consulting firm. Under her leadership, the firm has been named one of the Best Workplaces for Millennials by *Fortune* and Great Place to Work for four years in a row.

**ANNE SUGAR** is an executive coach and speaker who works with senior leaders in technology, marketing, and pharmaceutical companies. She is an executive coach for the Harvard Business School Executive Program and has guest-lectured at MIT. Find her at annesugar.com.

**RUCHIKA TULSHYAN** is the author of the book *Inclusion on Purpose: An Intersectional Approach to Creating a Culture of Belonging at Work* and the upcoming *Uncompete: Dismantling a Competition Mindset to Unlock Liberation, Opportunity, and Peace*. She is the founder of Candour, an inclusion strategy firm.

**LIZ WISEMAN** is the author of *Impact Players*, *Rookie Smarts*, and *Multipliers* and the CEO of the Wiseman Group. Connect with her on X/Twitter @LizWiseman.

**TIMOTHY YEN** is a clinical psychologist and consultant practicing in the San Francisco Bay area, who leads seminars and retreats around the globe. He is the author of the bestselling book *Choose Better: The Optimal Decision-Making Framework*. Between his years at Kaiser Permanente, in private practice, and in the U.S. Army as a Mental Health Staff Sergeant, he has empowered hundreds of individuals, families, organizations, and teams to develop authentic relationships and grow into their best selves.

# Accelerate your career with HBR's Work Smart Series.

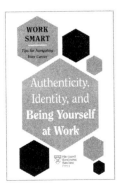
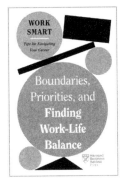

If you enjoyed this book and want more career advice from *Harvard Business Review*, turn to other books in **HBR's Work Smart Series**. Each title explores the topics that matter most to you as you start out in your career: being yourself at work, collaborating with (sometimes difficult) colleagues, maintaining your mental health, and more. **HBR's Work Smart Series** books are your go-to guides to step into and move forward successfully in your professional world.